Shout Because You're Free

Shout Because You're Free

The African American Ring Shout Tradition in Coastal Georgia

Text and Drawings by Art Rosenbaum

Photographs by Margo Newmark Rosenbaum

Musical Transcriptions and Historical Essay by Johann S. Buis

The University of Georgia Press | Athens and London

136388

Library of Congress Cataloging in Publication Data
Rosenbaum, Art.
     Shout because you're free : the African American ring shout tradition
in coastal Georgia / text and drawings by Art Rosenbaum; photographs by
Margo Newmark Rosenbaum ; musical transcriptions and historical essay
by Johann S. Buis.
          p.   cm.
     Includes bibliographical references and index.
     ISBN 0-8203-1934-1 (alk. paper)
     1. Afro-Americans—Georgia—McIntosh County—Social life and customs.
2. Afro-Americans—Georgia—McIntosh County—Religion.
3. Afro-Americans—Georgia—McIntosh County—Folklore.
4. McIntosh County (Ga.)—Social life and customs.   5. McIntosh County (Ga.)—
Religious life and customs.   6. Folklore—Georgia—McIntosh County.
I. Buis, Johann S.   II. Title.
F292.M15R67   1998
305.896′0730758737—dc21   97-43833

British Library Cataloging in Publication Data available

Frontis: *McIntosh County Shouters at Filming Session,* 1985

The publisher and the authors gratefully acknowledge the support of the Sapelo Foundation in the publication of this book.

Contents

Preface   *ix*

Acknowledgments   *xvii*

Introduction: "We Never Did Let It Go By"   *1*

1. "Kneebone in the Wilderness": The History of the Shout in America   *17*

2. "One Family of People": The Shouters of Bolden   *53*

3. Lawrence McKiver, Boss Songster   *85*

4. The Shout Songs   *105*

   Jubilee   *107*

   Blow, Gabriel   *110*

   Move for Your Dyin' Savior   *113*

   I Want to Die Like Weepin' Mary   *114*

   Wade the Water to My Knees   *116*

   Army Cross Over   *118*

   Happy Angel   *120*

   Move, Daniel   *121*

   Drive Ol' Joe   *124*

   I Come to Tell You   *126*

   Kneebone Bend   *127*

   Pharaoh's Host Got Lost   *130*

   Hold the Baby   *132*

   Religion, So Sweet   *134*

Time Drawin' Nigh (I See the Sign)   *137*

Read 'em, John   *139*

In This Field We Mus' Die   *142*

Eve and Adam   *144*

Went to the Burial (Sinner Rock So)   *146*

John on the Island, I Hear Him Groan   *150*

Walk through the Valley in the Field   *152*

Ezekiel Saw That Little Stone   *153*

Lay Down, Body   *155*

Watch That Star   *158*

Farewell, Last Day Goin'   *162*

Transcriber's Note   *164*

Historical Essay. The Ring Shout: Revisiting the Islamic and
African Issues of a Christian "Holy Dance"   *167*

Notes   *173*

Bibliography   *183*

Index   *189*

Preface

On a hot July afternoon in 1995, the annex building of the Mt. Calvary Baptist Church in Bolden, Georgia, did not ring with the sound of the shout songs or resound to the beating of a stick on the wood floor; nor did that floor move to the force of a score of people moving counterclockwise in the ring shout, as we had seen it on four Watch Night (or New Year's) shouts in the only community where the African American southeastern coastal ring shout is known to have survived. Instead, this day several members of the group that has become known as the McIntosh County Shouters were sitting down with us at long folding tables that usually hold church suppers, to go over the manuscript of *Shout Because You're Free*. Lawrence McKiver, patriarch and lead songster, was there along with Odessa Young, the oldest of the women who currently perform the compelling circling movements of the shout in public performance. A woman of great dignity, Odessa Young had overcome her reluctance to "talk" in order to help us tell the story of the shout correctly. Also there were Carletha Sullivan, a younger shouter who handles the business side of the tricky task of presenting a precious community tradition to the public, and Bettye Ector, an instructor at Coastal Georgia Community College in Brunswick, who is kin and neighbor to the shouters and who recently has become their presenter in public performances. Benjamin Reed, the "stick man," was there, as were shouters Vertie McIver and Venus McIver.

Though we had known the shouters of Bolden for sixteen years, we still needed to know how close we had come, in developing the manuscript, to "getting it right." Two shouters expressed some concern about the historical chapter, wondering whether readers might get bogged down in detail and annotations before getting into the story of the present-day shouters. We said we pretty much had to go with this section, as our publisher had urged us to locate the Bolden shout tradition in its broader context. We asked the members present about our attempts to convey a sense of the Gullah dialect through phonetic spellings, which had greatly concerned a folklorist who had earlier reviewed the manuscript; the spellings posed no problem for our consultants, who expressed pride in the "flat speech"—their term for the dialect of their parents and grandparents—and the elements of that speech which they retain. We did decide to follow the modern practice of avoiding dialectical respellings and spell all speech in standard English while retaining morphological elements as we heard them. We have chosen to retain some phonetic spellings in the song texts to better suggest the sound of the words carried by melody. Of more concern to Carletha and Bettye were typos and misspellings of "regular" English in the body of the manuscript, which we said we would attend to. Also of concern were incorrect spellings of names and place names in the community. For example, we had been told early on that the home of the shouters, a small community on the edge of Eulonia, was called "Bolden," and we spelled it that way in early publications of our field work. On a visit a few years ago, we saw a newly erected road sign reading "Bolton," and we assumed, incorrectly, that we had heard wrong earlier. Our consultants assured us that it was the road sign that was wrong—Bolden it is. (Now that sign is gone, but other newer ones marking side roads have been erected to honor Reverend Nathan Palmer, nonagenarian songster, and to recognize "Briar Patch," the slave cemetery that gives the community its other name.) Of greatest interest to our friends was that we more accurately describe the events and the roles of different individuals in the early 1980s when a group from the community formed to bring the shout to the public. There is an enormous pride in Bolden in having retained a tradition that, to their knowledge, has died out everywhere else, and in their well-received work outside the community during the past sixteen years of performing. We have tried to satisfy the shouters' requests while at the same time acknowledging that elements of the shout, and other closely related traditions, do endure elsewhere.

As it has developed, this book has assumed three voices: collectively, that of the shouters of Bolden, recounting their lives and their traditions in their own words; that of the author (for whose perceptions, interpretations, and lackings he alone is responsible); and that of history, gathered from the early reports of the shout through the observations and views of preachers, journalists, folklorists, and nonwitness commentators over the years. All these voices are interwoven, in perhaps an unconventional style, but I believe that it makes sense to follow a mid-nineteenth century account of a ring shout with a comparison to the shout in Bolden today, or to cautiously insert my own observation and commentary in a biographical section that is a largely verbatim interview. The reader will always know who is talking, and we hope that the layering of interview, exposition, and history will combine to provide an ultimately richer picture.

During our summer meeting with the shouters in 1995, we all looked at the images that would be a part of the book. Like most viewers who have seen my drawings of the shout, either in reproduction or exhibition, the shouters understand that these are not ethnographic documents; rather, the drawings are intended as sympathetic though subjective responses to the shout and its practitioners. While it is the present-day shouters and not their ancestors who are represented in the charcoal drawings, the subjects appreciate that I am trying to convey a sense of "time past in time present," not unlike the feeling the shouters bring to their performances. Margo Newmark Rosenbaum's photographs serve as a more faithful witness of time and place, recording the shout in the church annex on Watch Night, or the more stylized public performances. The photographs also appear in the form of portraits of the shouters and of views of their church and community. Margo's images stem from her personal view as well, with its subjective and artistic dimensions. Over the years she has shared her pictures with the shouters for both personal and publicity use. This transcultural image-making has been problematic at times. Still we are proud of our efforts and pleased that we have been invited to show the images at many venues, including the Gertrude Herbert Institute of Art in Augusta, Georgia, and the Avery Research Center for African American History and Culture at the

College of Charleston, where their reception has been positive. Yet we alone are responsible, as are all visual artists, for our images, as the work takes its place in the complex flux of cultural history.

Our greatest debt in the making of this book of course goes to the shouters of Bolden, who have welcomed us into their homes and church, and have shared patiently with us their personal histories and their most precious and time-honored traditions. Appreciation must be given also to many others who have helped in countless ways over the past sixteen years. Frankie and Doug Quimby were responsible for locating the shouters of Bolden, and as members of the Georgia Sea Island Singers and organizers of the Georgia Sea Island Festival, they provided insights into the history of bringing African American coastal traditions to the public. A conversation with Fred Hay first made us aware of the significance of the survival of the southeastern ring shout. Frank Ruzicka, former head of the University of Georgia Department of Art, helped in my visual and sound fieldwork through the University of Georgia Sea Grant Art Project. Our series of drawings and photographs relating to the shout was first exhibited in 1992 at the University of Georgia's Institute of Ecology gallery. A portion of the visual fieldwork was supported by an Individual Artist's Grant from the Georgia Council for the Arts. Some of the author's new drawings were exhibited at the council's Carriage Works Gallery in Atlanta in 1992. The drawings and photographs were expanded subsequently into an exhibition entitled "Shout!," which was organized by the Georgia Museum of Art and circulated throughout the Southeast. We appreciate the encouragement of Bill Eiland, Director of the museum, and the efforts of student curator James Bursenos in the realizing of this exhibition. The late Moe Asch, of Folkways Records, encouraged our efforts by issuing an LP of our field recordings of the shout songs; the author's notes to that release have been expanded into the present book. Clate Sanders of the Georgia Center for Continuing Education, supported by a grant from the Folk Arts Division of the National Endowment for the Arts, worked with us in the field to produce a half-hour television documentary on the McIntosh County Shouters. In 1987 the author worked with Allan E. MacLeod of the University of Georgia Henry W. Grady School of Journalism to make audio field recordings, which were produced as a radio series on Georgia folklore; coastal interview material from this project, supported by a grant from the Georgia Endowment for the Humanities, is included in the present work. We are appreciative of the encouragement and constructive comments of two University of Georgia colleagues, historian Bill McFeely, author of a rich study of the African American community near Bolden, on Sapelo Island; and John Garst, who, though his academic specialty is chemistry, is an authority on American folk hymnody. We have benefited greatly from pointed and thorough reports from outside readers who reviewed the manuscript. Our editor, and Director of the University of Georgia Press, Karen Orchard, has been untiringly supportive. The hard work of Jennifer Manley Rogers, project editor, Kim Cretors, copyeditor, and Kathi Dailey Morgan, designer, of the University of Georgia Press, was indispensable in making this book a reality. Special appreciation goes to ethnomusicologist Johann Buis, formerly Professor of Music in the School of Music, University of Georgia, currently coordinator of music education programs at the Center for Black Music Research, Columbia College, Chicago, for his hard work in transcribing the shout songs from our field recordings, and for his insightful essay on the music and its Afro-Arabic antecedents. We are greatly indebted to earlier field workers who have investigated the ring shout and related traditions on the southeastern coast, most important among them, William Francis Allen, Robert W. Gordon, Lydia Parrish, Guy and Candie Carawan, and Alan Lomax. We also have utilized the archival research of other scholars; in the interest of offering a full compendium of early reports of the shout, we reprint here considerable material found by Dena Epstein and published in her work, *Sinful Tunes and Spirituals: Black Folk Music to the Civil War* (1977).

Nearly all musical examples and interviews with the Bolden shouters have been transcribed from the author's audio tapes, made in field or public performance situations; a few interview segments were recorded by Clate Sanders of Georgia Public Television, or Allan E. MacLeod, working with the author. The original recordings have been deposited in the Archives of the Georgia Folklore Society in the University of Georgia Library. Some audio tapes that had been deteriorating have been preserved through grants obtained from Georgia Council for the Arts and the Sapelo Foundation by Linda Tadic, Head of Media, University of Georgia Libraries. The sounds and movement of the McIntosh County ring shout can best be appreciated by hearing and seeing them. *The McIntosh County Shouters:*

Slave Shout Songs from the Coast of Georgia, Folkways FE 4344, recorded and annotated by Art Rosenbaum, and the source for many of the transcribed performance songs in the present work, is currently available on special order in cassette or CD format from Smithsonian/Folkways Recordings, 955 L'Enfant Plaza SW, Suite 2600, MRC 914, Washington, DC 20560; telephone: (202) 287-3699. A half-hour television documentary, *Down Yonder: The McIntosh County Shouters*, produced by Clate Sanders with Art Rosenbaum, is available for purchase in VHS format from the Georgia Center Collection, Georgia Center for Continuing Education, Room 179, The University of Georgia, Athens, GA 30602; telephone: (800) 359-4040.

This book is not a work of ethnography or sociology. It is a study of a folk tradition in its community and historical context. Rather than to try to advance theory, the work is intended to document a tradition as we encountered it and to record what we hope will be the most complete history of the shout in the United States. One reader commented that it is not a scholarly work, though there is scholarly writing in it. That is about right—and the scholarly elements are here to provide context and support for the work's salient purposes—to record a substantial body of shout songs and information about the ring shout, much coming from the shouters of Bolden. I was frustrated in not being able to know more about "Billy"—the "great shouter" in the view of his fellows—whom nineteenth-century pioneer collector William Francis Allen observed, or about Lydia Parrish's informants earlier in this century. I am convinced that the fuller portrait of Lawrence McKiver will be of help to future students and scholars. It is hoped that the various textures of the book—the scholarly commentary, the music (even when committed to the printed page), the visual images, and the voices of the shouters of Bolden will combine to convey a sense of the beauty and power of the ring shout.

That July day in the annex, talk of business and manuscript revision wound down, and conversation moved to memories of the old days in the shout, when they had "the best" singers, basers, and shouters. Community and family life was more important then, and the women talked of the ring plays (secular counterparts of the shout) that they played as kids, "Sink, Titanic, in Jacksonville" and "Little Sally Walker"—games that today's kids don't play. But the shout endures, through both public performance and community practice. Benjamin Reed is still energized by the ancient rhythms moving through his stick—"I do it happy, get happy, shaking all over! You get to feeling good, especially if the song's set right, the shouters' shouting right, you can beat it!" And Vertie McIver says she feels, even as she speaks, the spirit of God that came to her as a child at the shout: "I can feel it right now. It's the same sweet, sweet spirit."

Acknowledgments

The McIntosh County Shouters

We, the McIntosh County Shouters, are blessed with a family of friends and supporters who contributed to our success.

We wish to thank our families for being there for us and giving us love and understanding—shouters like Deacon Andrew Palmer and Mrs. Lucille Holloway, now deceased, as well as Mrs. Oneitha Ellison, who paved the way so that our way might be easier.

We are eternally grateful to Deacon James Cook (deceased) for his vision—to broaden public awareness of "the shout" and its true meaning.

And we thank Mr. Robert Browning, director of the World Music Institute, for his continued interest and support in fostering cultural growth and development throughout the nation.

Introduction

"We Never Did Let It Go By"

The ring shout is the oldest African American performance tradition surviving on the North American continent. An impressive fusion of call-and-response singing, polyrhythmic percussion, and expressive and formalized dancelike movements, it has had a profound influence on African American music and religious practice. The integrity of the early form of the ring shout has survived in unbroken traditional practice from slavery times in the Bolden, or "Briar Patch," community in McIntosh County on the coast of Georgia. First described by outside observers in the mid-nineteenth century and practiced by slaves and their descendants principally in the coastal regions of South Carolina, Georgia, and Florida, the southeastern ring shout was believed to have died out in active practice by the middle of the twentieth century. Remarkably, the close-knit Bolden community and its Mount Calvary Baptist Church have continued the shout annually to welcome in the New Year on Watch Night. Since 1980 an organized group from the community has also performed the shout away from home at churches, folk festivals, and universities, and this has reinforced local pride in the venerable practice. "The only people can shout is right here," shouter Catherine Campbell affirms. "Calvary was the stopping place of the shout because we kept the tradition going. We never did let it go by."

Lydia Parrish collected shout songs in McIntosh County and published them in *Slave Songs of the Georgia Sea Islands* (1942). The shout also had survived near her home on St. Simons Island in Glynn County, just south of McIntosh; but her informants there were self-conscious about performing the shout for her, and it was "years before [she] was permitted to see the Sea Island Negroes indulge in this innocent pastime" (Parrish, 54). Yet Parrish was to some extent aware of the long history of discouragement of the shout by white missionaries and some individuals in the black clergy. The Georgia Sea Island Singers were organized by Parrish in order to perpetuate slave-song traditions, including the shout songs, through public performance even as the ring shout was fading in local practice. In 1980 Frankie and Doug Quimby of the Sea Island Singers and organizers of the Sea Island Festival heard reports of a community in McIntosh County where Watch Night shouts were still being held to the beat of a broom on a wood floor. With the help of folklorists Fred Fussell and George Mitchell, the Quimbys located the shouters of Bolden, who were persuaded to form a group that would present the traditional practice at the festival on St. Simons that year.

We were among those who saw the group, which was assembled by Lawrence McKiver, first perform the ring shout for the public on a wooden stage under the huge live oak trees; all the elements of this presumed extinct tradition were presented conscientiously, much as the elements had been reported by nineteenth-century observers. McKiver, as lead singer or "songster," began or "set" a song. At his side sat a "sticker" or "stick man," beating a broomstick on the floor in rhythm. Behind them a group of other singers, or "basers," answered McKiver's lines in call-and-response fashion, at the same time setting up counter-rhythms to the stick beat with clapping hands and patting feet. Then the "shouters," women dressed in the long dresses and head rags of their grandmothers' day, began to move in a counterclockwise circle, with a compelling hitching shuffle, often stooping or extending their arms in gestures pantomiming the content of the song being sung. This looked like dancing, but nonagenarian Deacon James Cook later explained the difference: "Back in the days of my coming on in the shout, if you cross your feet you were dancing, but if you solid, move on the square, you were shouting. But if you cross your feet you were turned out of the church because you were doing something for the devil. . . . So you see those ladies didn't cross their feet, they shouted! And shouting is . . . praising God with an order of thanksgiving."[1]

Like their slave ancestors, today's shouters apply the term "shout" specifically to the movements rather than to the vocal or accompanying percussive components of the shout tradition, and distinguish between shouters— those who step and move in the ring—and the singers, basers, and stickers. Lorenzo Dow Turner reported that the word is a Gullah dialect survival of the Afro-Arabic *saut*, sometimes pronounced "shout," meaning a fervent dance around the Kabaa in Mecca.[2] In his essay concluding the present work, ethnomusicologist Johann Buis advances the discussion of the relationships between the Arabic *saut* and the coastal ring shout. Early on, practitioners of the shout may have had their concept of the shout as a way to praise God reinforced by the English word "shout" in the Psalms ("O clap your hands, all ye people, shout unto God," Ps. 47:1) and elsewhere in Scripture; the Afro-Arabic *saut* does incorporate song as well as movement. Thus it is understandable that outside commentators should confuse shout as movement with the English word for a loud vocalization. Historical accounts of the coastal ring shout, as well as the testimony of the shouters of Bolden whom we have interviewed, usually differentiate between the shout as movement and the singing and percussive rhythm, even as they might refer to the collective components of the practice as "the shout." In inland areas where the ring shout has been forgotten, the term "shout" is still commonly used to describe the violent movements rather than the vocalization of a worshiper seized by the Spirit.

The shouters of Bolden also clearly differentiate between the shout songs and other types of religious songs, such as spirituals, hymns, and the more recent jubilee and gospel songs. The shout songs (in earlier times occasionally referred to as "runnin' spirituals") begin slowly at times but quickly accelerate to the brisk tempo of the shout. Most of them date back to slavery times, and many of the melodies hint at African and Afro-Caribbean origins. The texts, while occasionally prosaic and even secular ("Hold the Baby"), carry biblical messages ("Pharaoh's Host Got Lost"), coded references to the hardships of slavery ("Move, Daniel"), and often rise to impressive heights of apocalyptic poetry ("Time Drawin' Nigh"). Perhaps the texts function to mobilize those who perform the shout into the group-affirming symbolic motion; this may explain the positive content of the shout song texts, even when the subject is confrontation with death ("Wade the Water to My Knees"), when compared to the more poignant, introspective sentiments frequently expressed in early spirituals some of which have been called "sorrow songs."

Another defining element of the shout tradition, at least in the coastal regions of Georgia, Florida, and South Carolina, is that it has almost never been a regular part of church worship service but takes place in churches only after the prayer meeting is over. Some members of the clergy were sympathetic to the practice and others opposed it. The southeastern coastal ring shout, unlike a related tradition, the singing and praying bands in the Chesapeake Bay region,[3] has functioned outside of the structured worship of the organized church. In earlier times benches were pushed out of the way in the church so that the shout might have room to proceed; or shouters would meet surreptitiously in cabins or in "praise houses" in the woods. In recent years churches have been modernized, the pews have been fixed to the floor, and the floors carpeted; Deacon Cook spoke sadly of such "dead churches with a concrete floor."[4] However the Mount Calvary church congregation has built an annex with a wooden floor to allow room for shouting and for the resonance of the stick. The shout is also seasonal—as Deacon Cook put it, "shouting ain't no easy job. The tradition of shouting is when it was cold weather." This meant the Christmas to New Year's holiday season within the memories of today's shouters. Vertie McIver recalls that as she was growing up, the community would have shouts from house to house during Christmas week, go to church to shout on Christmas, and finally go to Mount Calvary on New Year's; they would "shout all night long," beginning at midnight and shouting until day break when they would sing "Farewell, Last Day Goin'."

Though there is ongoing debate about the degree of African origination of many African American folk traditions, there is little question, both from internal evidence and from the testimony of today's inheritors of the shout tradition, that the basic elements of the ring shout were brought from Africa. Besides the term itself, the call-and-response singing, the polyrhythms of the stick and hands and feet, the swaying and hitching shuffle of the shouters, all derive from African forms. The fusion of dance, song, and rhythm in fervid religious possession is an African practice, and it is not surprising that the ring shout flourished in coastal areas where there are many other documented examples of African, including Afro-Arabic, survivals.

White camp-meeting songs also utilized call-and-response and white sects, such as the Shakers, worshipped in moving circles, but exposure of blacks to these white practices does not negate the African origins of the shout, though it might suggest a reinforcement or modification of African-derived practices. Deacon Cook stated explicitly that his forebears, born in slavery, told him that their ancestors had brought the shout off the ship from Africa in the 1700s. Lawrence McKiver's family tradition has it that "Kneebone Bend" was a shout performed as the family's slave ancestors landed in Virginia. McKiver understood that the slaves were not Christian when they arrived in America and that the tradition had to have evolved in practice in the New World; as he put it, while the shout moves "to an African beat . . . the slave, after he got over here, they got a little bit more—time brings on a change—they could get hold a little bit of the Bible, that's the way they tell me, and the one that could learn to read a little bit, they could . . . pick out a word, and they make—that's the way they make the songs." The slaves adapted their dialect of the English language, Christianity, and some elements of the musical traditions and hymnody encountered in America to the African-derived shout forms.

Since the first thrilling encounter with the living shout tradition on St. Simons, we have visited the Bolden community numerous times—recording the shout songs and other traditions, interviewing many members of the community, and attending four Watch Night shouts. We have observed the performing group that came to be known as the McIntosh County Shouters at such venues as the National Folk Festival at Wolf Trap Farm and the Georgia Folklife Festival in Atlanta, and have begun to appreciate the artistic triumphs as well as the internal conflicts and dissensions that have arisen as the shout tradition was recontextualized as public performance. We disseminated material from this fieldwork, first in a Folkways LP, *The McIntosh County Shouters: Slave Shout Songs from the Coast of Georgia* (FE 4344, currently available as a Smithsonian Folkways cassette), and then as a Georgia Public Television documentary, *Down Yonder—The McIntosh County Shouters* (produced by Clate Sanders in 1987). Our intention with this book is to expand our study of the southeastern coastal ring shout in the only community in which it is known to have survived. Certainly a pivotal question will be why the shout has persisted in Bolden long after it died out elsewhere and the conditions for its perpetuation had been presumed to belong to a distant past. The answer will come in large part from

Lawrence McKiver, James Cook, Nathan Palmer, Doretha Skipper, and many other shouters of Bolden who have been generous in sharing their treasured traditions and insights with us, and who will tell their stories in their own words. We will document the history of the shout in the United States and trace its African and Caribbean origins insofar as this can be done. We will attempt to discover how the shout tradition may have changed as it moved from practice totally sustained within a tiny folk community into public performance for audiences far from home. And we will ask: Have the stubborn bearers of this tradition changed in their artistic and personal relationships vis-à-vis the shout now that they have been applauded at the Smithsonian and been honored by a National Folk Heritage Award?

As outsiders looking at the shout tradition and interacting in various ways with the Bolden community, we have gradually learned that we are not detached observers of a relatively self-contained and self-perpetuating cultural manifestation; rather we are part of the continuing story of the shout as a paradigm of traditional African culture redefining itself in the New World, frequently in the view of, and at times subject to, the attitudes of white (and black) outsiders. Some of these outsiders have denounced the shout as heathenish, others have admired it mainly as an interesting cultural artifact; we are among those others who have seen the shout as a proud assertion of human spirit and supportive community over the degradations of slavery and oppression. We have come to see the shout not only as a magnificent art form but also as a social force. Our tools in documenting and interpreting the shout have been not only tape recorder, pencil, and video camera, but still camera and sketch pad. A body of visual work—photographs and large finished drawings derived from on-the-spot sketches and photo and video sources—has come out of our years of research of the shout. Some of these photographs and drawings are included here, and it is hoped that they will add a seen dimension to the understanding of a performance tradition in which visual expression and movement in time are as important as text, melody, and rhythm. Finally, we will present a substantial body of shout songs as they have survived in the Bolden community.

Watch Night Shout, 1994

The Georgia Coast is a region of river mouths and inlets, barrier islands and salt marshes; it angles northeast from the Florida line past

Brunswick up to the old colonial port city of Savannah, which lies along the Savannah River just below South Carolina. McIntosh County is at the approximate midpoint of the coast. Late in the afternoon on New Year's Eve 1994, we enter the county on the highway running arrow-straight from the West, through the monotonous scrub-pine landscape of the Georgia coastal plain. Our destination is the Bolden Community on the mainland; it is on the outskirts of the small town of Eulonia. We drive through the crossroad town of Townsend. Up a side road is Ardock, home of Jim Cook who died at the age of 103 after a life "in the shout." Abruptly the road enters the cluster of motels at the Eulonia interchange of Interstate 95, then crosses the old north-south coastal highway. A mile farther we pass a driveway leading into an overgrown property under a rusted metal double arch; framed by the arch are cut-out letters reading "The Forest." This is the plantation where the slave forebears of the shouters of Bolden toiled for the Wylly family. Under this sign another reads, "SAY NO TO DRUGS." Then we enter the Bolden community of modest houses set back from the main road and along several dirt and paved side roads that wind under the trees. Out of sight a mile to the north is the Sapelo River, flowing from the swamp into the Sapelo Sound. Here, except for some old wooden fishing boats propped up for restoration beside one house, there is little to indicate that we are in a coastal region; a few miles farther down the road this would change, with bluffs overlooking the salt marshes coming into view, then the shrimp fleet at dock in Meridian, the boat landing to Sapelo Island, and finally the great Altamaha River flowing to the sea by the county seat town of Darien. We stop to talk to a few people gathered in the sandy yard of Mount Calvary Baptist Church, including Sister Doretha Skipper and Rev. Leonard Jackson. Sister Skipper tells us that the shout will go on tonight, even though there has just been a funeral for the sister of Lawrence McKiver. Rev. Leonard Jackson performed the funeral service. Pastor for just three years, he is eagerly anticipating his first Watch Night shout; a resident of Jacksonville, Florida, he missed the shouts the last two years. He mentions having seen the television documentary of the shout in Bolden, and seems impressed that this celebrated tradition survives among his flock.

As the last brilliant winter sun of 1993 is etching the Spanish moss hanging from massive live oaks along a road a few hundred yards from the church, Rev. Nathan Palmer, a great songster in his day, is splitting wood in his yard. He tells us he will be ninety-four if he lives until next June 4. On previous visits he declined to be interviewed, this stance seeming to confirm the suggestion by some in the community that he preferred to keep information about the shout within the community and was unenthusiastic about those who performed the shout away from home for the public. This evening he is cordial but continues to be somewhat reticent; he will not explain why the shout has survived here but does mention that one pastor tried to stop it—and it "wasn't long 'fore he was gone!" He says he will not be at the upcoming shout, and lets us know that he is content to leave others to carry on the shout. He goes back to his work.

Back off the main road, Lawrence McKiver has returned home after his sister's funeral. After we offer condolences, he talks about his family, all singers and shouters, and the shouts they used to have at Prospect Baptist Church and New Homes Baptist Church: "all them churches dropped the shout, but Calvary never dropped it." McKiver brings up a recent schism in the performing group, which is painful, as the breakaway faction includes friends and kin. As he begins to clean fish that will be fried that night, he reaffirms his belief that the songs have to be sung right, and with the proper understanding of their meaning. "Anybody sing a song, ain't got a taste to it, it's like food without salt." Two animated men come in the back door. They are Harold Evans, a singer and clapper, and Benjamin Reed, stick man, stalwarts of McKiver's "crew." As they begin to help clean the fish in the kitchen, we continue our conversation with McKiver in his sparsely furnished bedroom. He tells us, "These men in there, they want things to go right on."

Prayer meeting begins at the church shortly after 10:00 P.M. with the spiritual "You Brought Me from a Mighty Long Way." Thoughts are on the passage of time from one year to the next, from birth to death, in the words of the next song:

I could have been dead and in my grave,
I'm glad to be in that number one more time.

A chanted prayer continues the theme: "Thank you for bringing us on another twelve mile journey." Then Deacon Freddie Palmer sings:

You gotta run, you gotta run,
All God's chillun got a race to run.

Meet me, Jesus, meet me,
Meet me in the middle of the air.

No theological abstractions here, but rather the stark imagery of "getting over":

First time I went down in the water,
It rose up above my knees.

Second time I went down in the water,
It rose up above my waist,

Third time I went down in the water,
It rose up above my head.
Jesus on the other side
He was makin' up my dying bed.

Members pray, testify, and lead spirituals as the feeling comes to them. Lawrence McKiver sings "Lord Guide My Feet While I Run This Race." Gospel songs of more recent vintage follow the older spirituals. Reverend Jackson then invites the associate pastors to deliver "sermonettes," and he reminds the congregation of the approach of midnight and the New Year. Reverend Bryant's sermon flows into the spiritual "God's Angels Watchin' over Me," and he asks, "Why do I sing and shout like I do?" The excitement builds as the choir sings "Get on Board, Get Right This Way." Finally Reverend Jackson preaches the old year out and the New Year in:

"It's *midnight* when I see young kids toting guns to school!" His text is the wise and foolish virgins, and he exhorts the congregation to "get some oil in your lamp." The familiar call-and-response pattern is intensified, as he repeatedly asks for affirmation: "Can I get a witness?" At midnight, by pre-arrangement, the lights are cut off and the congregation kneels in prayer. Then the lights come on, everyone shakes hands and embraces, and the spiritual "Another New Year" is raised.

This concludes the prayer meeting; countless similar ones will have taken place this night in traditional black churches across the South and beyond. But at Mount Calvary, the excitement does not wind down with the congregants talking and driving away home into the dark New Year or lingering for some fellowship and refreshment. Here everyone knows that there will be shout in the annex, and people move there through a passageway past the baptismal font or leave the church's main entrance and enter the annex. The annex is a plain, oblong room with lights and fans hanging from a low stucco ceiling and is furnished with folding chairs and tables used for church suppers; a kitchen is off the back.

Before long the room is crowded, as it had been when we first attended a Watch Night shout in 1982. The formal presentation we had seen of McKiver's group on festival stages had not prepared us for the energy, intensity, and seeming disorganization of the shout in community practice as we witnessed it in 1982. Food was quickly passed from the kitchen, and people talked and mingled. Soon, above the din, came the beat of the stick on the wooden floor and the strains of "Move, Daniel." The singers and stick beaters did not stay in one place but moved in a fluid fashion around the room. A ring of shouters snaked among people who were eating and conversing. Absent were the old-fashioned dresses and overalls the group wore in their public performances; people wore a variety of modern clothing. Nobody seemed to mind the informality, and at times the singing rose to extraordinary heights of feeling. Reverend Palmer was there that year and was persuaded to sing by chants of "just one for the New Year, Rev'!" His singing of the shout song "Time Drawin' Nigh" was one of the most soul-stirring and masterful performances of African American traditional singing I have experienced. Later McKiver told me that we had not seen an ideal performance of the shout that night. People who had moved away from the community and were visiting for the holidays and others not schooled in the tradition had inhibited proper execution of the shout. He further assured me that the stage presentations by his group at folk festivals were faithful presentations of the shouts as they knew them in their youth, when standards of performance were more strictly observed. When we returned on Watch Night of 1986, we had permission to film the shout for the Georgia Public Television documentary. Although efforts were made to be as unobtrusive as possible, lights, camera, and microphone booms intruded. The shout went off well regardless with those in attendance taking the film crew rather in stride. At the third Watch Night shout we attended, in 1992, members of the organized performing group had chosen to be "in costume," the women wearing the matching long dresses and bonnets, the men wearing the overalls and work shirts they wear in stage performances; the others in attendance wore whatever modern dress was appropriate for the prayer meeting. The shout was well performed and space was kept clear for those in the ring. In 1986 Catherine Campbell got together a "children's shout" and instructed them in the shout for the cameras. In 1992 there seemed to be considerable interest on the part of the children; several tried to learn to beat the stick from their elders.

This night, in 1994, children are clearly eager to participate as the shout begins. Lawrence McKiver and Benjamin Reed lay down a plywood board they have been using for a few years for added resonance from the stick, and McKiver "sets" the first shout song, "Jubilee." He is addressing the children who are lined up—much as if they were waiting to board a school bus—with the song he dates from the Emancipation, repeating the line: "Shout my children 'cause you're free!" The children move into the circle, imitating the older people in the ring. Their execution does not have the control or style that we have been shown repeatedly by the older shouters as being the proper way to shout, but spirits are high, and no one discourages them or corrects their efforts. I recall McKiver's memory of the old sisters of his youth: "Folks who wouldn't do the shout properly and try to bop them while they going, they would shove that one out of the ring, maybe a youngster, push him to the side . . . let him *watch* until he catch on to how it go, to keep from bucking the ring shout, you see. 'Cause them sisters would be in them long dresses and stuff, and when they doing that shout they want to do it *perfect*, and they's going to stay in that circle, and they's gonna move directly to that shout. Every time the song change, *they* change. When the song say 'rock,' they do a rock, if it say 'shout,' they do a level shout, and that's just the way they do it. If you can't do it, well, you can't participate with them. You got to move out of the way."

In 1994 there is no pushing of children, or for that matter of adults, who are not shouting in the most traditional way, out of the ring. But gradually as the night goes on, they drop out on their own, and more of the shouters are older women and men, experienced shouters. They move with controlled body movements, the elbows usually slightly bent, and the torso leaning gently in the direction of the forward motion. Their steps are small, measured, shuffling; feet never cross. This is the classic shout step, described by Bess Lomax Hawes as a "rapid shuffling two-step, the back foot closing up to but never passing the leading foot: step (R), close (L); step (R), close (L)."[5] The lead foot always advances to the beat of the stick on the principal accents of the rhythm; at times the lead is shifted to the other foot. The shouters know the songs, and they move not only to the rhythm but also to the meaning of the verses. When "Eve and Adam" is sung, they make gestures of gathering leaves "in the Garden," and in "Move, Daniel," they extend their arms in winglike positions when the verse is sung:

Do the eagle wing, Daniel,
Do the eagle wing, Daniel!

They understand that this song was sung in slavery, and Daniel was a slave being urged to fly from the master's whip. While the shouters maintain even control, the knot of singers and stickers pick up in intensity as the night goes on. Lawrence McKiver leads most of the songs, but Freddie Palmer and others lead occasionally. Doretha Skipper, a good leader, stays among the basers this night.

Fried fish and boiled shrimp and crab are brought from the kitchen, and there is cake and tea. Tonight there is no "hoppin' John," the traditional black-eyed peas-and-rice dish that is usually served on Watch Night. Slowly the crowd thins out, but the shouters and singers carry on energetically. Songs that have been sung earlier in the evening—"Kneebone Bend," "Believer, I Know," and "Lay Down, Body"—are repeated, some for the third time, as if to improve on the execution of the shout now that the room is not as crowded and the more experienced shouters are in the ring.

Eventually, near three o'clock in the morning, the singers and shouters begin to tire. They call up energy for the song favored in recent years to conclude Watch Night, "Farewell, Last Day Goin'":

I hate to leave you,
    Farewell, last day goin', farewell!
I had a good time,
    Farewell, last day goin', farewell!
I hope to see you,
    Farewell, last day goin', farewell!
Another time,
    Farewell, last day goin', farewell!

The New Year has been shouted in, but not its dawn, which is unlike the Watch Night shouts remembered from the youth of today's elder shouters when people shouted all night long. As the last few people in the annex prepare to leave, someone starts the old spiritual, "Another New Year" that had been sung earlier in the church:

It's another New Year, oh, and I ain't gone,
It's another New Year, oh, and I ain't gone,
It's another New Year, oh, and I ain't gone.
Thank God a-mighty that I ain't gone.

Though the shout has not lasted all night long, it has been the best-attended, most vigorous, and most passionate of the four we have attended. The old shout songs have been sung with intensity by several excellent singers, and the ring shout has been performed by elder shouters and younger members of the community bent on learning and participating. A few weeks later, shouter Carletha Sullivan would comment that this evening was much "like it used to be." The persistence of this ancient and moving tradition in the last decade of the twentieth century, barely two miles from Interstate 95, is one of the amazing survivals of American folklife.[6]

Shout Because You're Free

1 "Kneebone in the Wilderness"

The History of the Shout in America

Anyone who had slaves they collected them all together and took them to
the places called Aladabara and Jufufe to sell them to the Portuguese.

Then the Portuguese put them in their ship and left there and went to
Jang Jang Bure.

When they left there they went right to the slave house to collect the
slaves there and take them to the Dutch.

Then the Dutch collected them and sent them to America.

It is because of this that slaves were plenty in America.

They called them American Negroes.

—from *Toolong jang,* sung by West African griot

Alhaji Fabala Kanuteh

By the late nineteenth century it was too late for African religion—and
therefore for African culture—to be contained or reversed because its
advocates were practically the entire black population in America. The
essential features of the ring shout were present in one form or another,
and hardly a state in the Union was without its practitioners following
slavery. Moreover, the shout continued to be the principal context in
which creativity occurred.

—Sterling Stuckey, *Slave Culture*

According to Lawrence McKiver, "every bit of it is an African act. The old people, that's what they tell me. Nobody does it but our kind of people. The shout . . . it's just an African act. You can tell by the singing, tell by the song, tell by the beat, it's actually an African beat. I think they come in 1722 when the blacks came over here. It came down through the generations. It used to be real popular one time. But it fall on back, fall on back. I don't think no others got it, that I know of."

"They brought it [the shout] here with them. My people," said old Jim Cook. Lawrence McKiver is specific about the song they brought, "Knee-bone Bend," and the dancelike movement that went with it: "That's the oldest slave song that ever was sung by black people when they first come over from Africa over here. See, the song would say 'kneebone in the wilderness,' you see, they didn't know where they was—so that was going to a place they . . . didn't know nothing about, understand? So they would sing this song, 'kneebone in the wilderness, kneebone in the valley,' they was praying at the time, that's why they say 'kneebone bend,' they was bending down, they was praying. . . . That's the way my mama told it to me, and aunts. I had some old ancestors that put out these songs, you know."[1] This oral testimony brings into focus a poignant image of the very moment of the disembarkment of African slaves in the New World. The act of kneeling has significance in the African tradition as well as in European Christianity.[2] The bent-knee posture in African dance and art "signaled the presence of supple life energies."[3] In the present day shout, the song text recalling supplication, and the bent-knee posture of the shouters as they move actively around the ring, unites the more receptive supplication and the active expression of life-affirming energy.

A history of the African roots of the shout must begin with the earliest reports of African dancing, particularly dancing in the service of religion, contemporaneous with the slave trade. Robert Farris Thompson cited Ten Thyne's account of dancing in southern Africa in 1673: "They take the greatest delight in dancing. . . . If they have the least feeling for religion, it is in the observation of the dance that they must show it . . . with their bodies leaning forward, stamp on the ground vigorusly with their feet, lustily chanting in unison . . . and with a fixed expression on their faces."[4] Thompson relates this description, particularly as it concerns stance and posture, to a modern description of Bushmen dancing to the Southwest of the Cape in the Kalahari: "the ceremonial dance [is] a religious act, but, although very serious . . . is not piously solemn or constrained and it provides occasion for pleasure and aesthetic satisfaction . . . the men dance with knees bent and bodies carried with little motion, leaning forward. The steps are very precise. They are minute in size, advancing only two or three inches, but they are strongly stamped, and ten or twenty dancers stamping together produces a loud thud."[5] This last description parallels the movements of the shout as practiced today in McIntosh County, especially the small steps and incremental forward motion as well as the leaning stance.

One might speculate that there may have been some influence of Native American practices in the development of the ring shout. From the first arrival of slaves from Africa and the Caribbean to the Southeast, there was contact between blacks and Native American peoples. Escaped slaves lived near and among the Seminoles of Florida. During the war with U.S. authorities in the 1830s, these blacks were allies of the Seminoles; when captured, some were returned to their owners to the North, others went West to live with deported Seminoles as free persons or slaves.[6] In 1992, some "black Seminoles" from Texas met the McIntosh County Shouters of Bolden on a Black Arts Festival stage in Atlanta; the Texans recalled Watch Night shout traditions of their youth, which were closely related to the shouts of the Georgia coast. At some time there may have been some influence of the vocal, rhythmic, and dance traditions of the southeastern Indians on the African Americans. We have seen African characteristics in the shout movement, yet it is not unlike some aspects of Native American dance. An early twentieth-century description of the Seminole corn dance states that "for men, the dance is the characteristic double step of the Indian Dance."[7] And Frank W. Speck has described the dancing of the Yuchis, an Oklahoma people whose origin was along the border of Georgia and South Carolina, and who in the Southeast had held slaves and were of mixed blood: "The movement was from right to left, contra-clockwise. The steps of the dancers were short, the motion being chiefly in the leg below the knee. In general effect the dance steps look more like shuffling."[8] Certainly counterclockwise circle dancing is characteristic of many cultures, but whether the similarities in the characteristic Native American double step and the shuffling "two step" of the ring shout are causal or coincidental awaits further study.

Moving in a counterclockwise circle is characteristic of African dance, though as we have noted is not confined to African practice. Elaine Nichols notes that similar forms to African circle dances were called ring shouts or plantation walk-arounds in black American culture. In Africa they were essential in rituals honoring the dead. . . . Robert F. Thompson and Sterling Stuckey offer a clue to the importance of moving in a circle around the grave. The grave is the most sacred point upon which a person can take an oath or affirm that "life is a shared process with the dead below the river or the sea." "Drawing or signing a point" on the ground summons the power of God and the ancestors. It is not inconceivable that the ring shout or counterclockwise movement around the grave represented such an oath or statement for Africans in the New World. This is especially true when one considers Thompson's statement that when combined with singing, marking the point causes the power of God to descend upon that exact spot.

Nichols further suggests that "used in this fashion, the ring shout is suggestive of a form of 'ground writing' or drawing symbols on the ground as a means of communicating with God and the ancestors."[9] Thompson describes the cosmogram of Kongo culture as a circle with four points signifying the four moments of the sun, "the continuity of human life" with "God . . . at the top, the dead at the bottom, and water in between."[10] While one must be cautious about connecting all Afro-Atlantic counterclockwise circle dances with this cosmogram, Thompson does draw a parallel between the "mystic ground-drawings in Cuba" and "the development of Afro-Christian crosses, chalked on the floor as critical 'points' among the Trinidad Shouters."[11] And Nichols's association of circle dances with funerals is substantiated on the Georgia coast with the account of slave funerals by ex-slave Ben Sullivan of St. Simons Island: "Now, ole man Dembo he use tuh beat huh drum tuh duh fewnul, but Mr. Couper he stop dat. He say he dohn wahn drums beatin roun duh dead. But I watch em hab a fewnul. I gits behine duh bush an hide an see what dey does. Dey go in a long pruhcession tuh duh buryin ground an dey beat duh drums long duh way an dey submit duh body tuh duh groun. Den dey dance roun in a ring an dey motion wid duh hans. Dey sing duh body tuh duh grabe an den dey let it down an den dey succle roun in duh dance."[12]

Harold Courlander cites this and similar accounts as putting to rest "any doubt that . . . 'shouting' was in reality dancing."[13] He further surmises that New Orleans funeral processions to the accompaniment of brass bands grew out of the practice of drum beating in funeral processions.

Even before death, a circle dance around a dying person was evidently an African practice surviving in slave culture. "Aunt Fanny," a Virginia cook and devout Christian, permitted, in the words of her horrified mistress, "Negroes . . . to perform their religious rites around [her] death bed. Joining hands they performed a savage dance, shouting wildly around the bed. This was horrible to hear and see, especially as in this family every effort had been made to instruct their negro dependants in the truths of religion. . . . After the savage dance and rites were over . . . I went and said to her 'we are afraid the noise and dancing have made you worse.'

"Speaking feebly, she replied: 'Honey, that kind of religion suits us black folks better than your kind.'"[14]

Today's shouters of Bolden have not ascribed any special symbolic meaning to the counterclockwise circle, nor do they recall the shout or any dancelike movement being made before death or in funerals. They do clearly regard the shout as a way of honoring God and of evoking at the very least thoughts of departed ancestors and are thus not far removed from significances deeply embedded in their practices, meanings linking them with African tradition and belief. Sterling Stuckey considers the slave ring shout to be "above all, devoted to the ancestral spirits, to reciprocity between the living and the dead."[15]

Though the component elements of the shout are African and the oral tradition of today's shouters is unequivocal about the African origin of the shout, we can never know precisely what form of the evolving tradition was practiced by the first slaves in America. Christian elements were absent, as the slaves were Christianized later; the Gullah dialect had yet to develop; drums were likely to have been used, but we cannot guess what other percussive intruments may have been used, besides clapping and foot tapping that could be produced by the human body. As the slaves were Christianized in the late eighteenth century and during the Great Revival Period of the early nineteenth century, the African practices we call the shout fused with the religious orientation of the newly converted slaves. Albert J. Raboteau has described this fusion of African practice and Protestant revivalism:

> In the ring shout and allied patterns of ecstatic behavior, the African heritage of dance found expression in the evangelical religion of the American slaves. To be sure, there are significant differences between the kind of spirit possession found in West Africa and in the shouting

experience of American revivalism. Different theological meanings are expressed and experienced in each. But similar patterns of response—rhythmic clapping, ring-dancing, styles of singing, all of which reveal the slaves' African religious background. The shout is a convincing example of [Melville] Herskovits' theory of reinterpretation of African traditions; for the situation of the camp-meeting revival, where enthusiastic and ecstatic religious behavior was encouraged, presented a congenial setting for slaves to merge African patterns of response with Christian interpretations of the experience of spirit possession, an experience shared by both blacks and whites. The Protestant revivalist tradition, accepted by the slaves and their descendants in the United States, proved in this instance to be amenable to the influence of African styles of behavior. Despite the prohibition of dancing as heathenish and sinful, the slaves were able to reinterpret and "sanctify" their African tradition of dance in the "shout." While North American slaves danced under the impulse of the Spirit of a "new" God, they danced in ways their fathers in Africa would have recognized. The "holy dance" of the shout may very well have been a two-way bridge connecting the core of West African religions—possession by the gods—to the core of evangelical Protestantism—experience of conversion.[16]

Certainly Raboteau is correct in seeing the fervor of the Protestant revivalism as a catalyst for the adaptation of African religious practices to Christian worship, yet there was another current in the movement to Christianize the slaves that ran counter to African-derived traditions. In slavery times the shout was often practiced clandestinely, as white and black clergy often disapproved of it (although it has been suggested that black preachers at times publicly disapproved of the shout while they were more supportive of its practice away from the eyes of white observers). In an early description of the ring shout, William Francis Allen quoted an article from the *New York Nation* of May 30, 1867, which called the shout "a ceremony which the white clergymen are inclined to discountenance, and even some of the colored elders . . . try sometimes to put on a face of discouragement."[17] It was not only the ring shout and the songs associated with it, but also other black spirituals that were suppressed by white missionaries, such as Charles Colcock Jones, who were attempting to instill more orthodox forms of worship into the beliefs of converted slaves. In Liberty County, Georgia (just to the north of McIntosh County) in the 1840s, Jones found the slave songs "too African, dangerously extravagant," according to Erskine Clarke. "And perhaps . . . he heard hidden within these songs both resistance to subordination and profound spiritual insights that cut through his pretensions, that his own heart could not face. . . . At any rate, Jones rejected them all and sought to replace them with the hymns of white Protestantism. 'One great advantage,' he had told the planters, 'in teaching them good psalms and hymns, is that they are thereby induced to lay aside the extravagant and nonsensical chants, and catches and hallelujah songs of their own composing; and when they sing . . . they will have something profitable to sing.'" [18] Jones disapproved of "boistrous singing immediately at the close" of divine worship. [19] This stricture may well have been directed specifically at the singing of shout songs and the ring shout, which were typically practiced after formal worship services.

At an earlier time, before the Great Revival period of the nineteenth century, secular music and dance among the slaves were encouraged frequently by the slave owners, at times coupled with discouragement of religious practice. [20] In a climate in which ring dances and musical instruments were permitted, it is plausible to expect African religious forms to survive in vigorous practice up to the time when such attitudes as Jones's strove to eliminate or marginalize those forms. A former slave described Carolina plantation life at the beginning of the nineteenth century where some slaves practiced Mohamedanism, others professed polytheism—all this along with "singing, playing on the banjoe, and dancing." Yet on Sunday, there was a meeting with (Christian) singing and prayer, although many slaves went searching for fruit instead. [21]

It is not surprising that the shout, growing out of ongoing Afro-Atlantic practices, could survive and continue to develop in a form resilient enough to withstand pressures of the religious orthodoxy of Jones's time. Harold Coulander considers the shout

> a fusion of two seemingly irreconcilable attitudes toward religious behavior. In most of Africa, dance, like singing and drumming, is an integral part of supplication. Not all religious rites in West Africa include dancing, but most of them do. . . . Among West Africans, dancing in combination with other elements is regarded as a form of appeal to supernatural forces, and this tradition remains alive in New World

African cults in Haiti, Jamaica, Trinidad, and other West Indian islands. In the Euro-Christian tradition, however, dancing in church is generally regarded as a profane act. The ring shout in the United States provides a scheme which reconciles both principles. The circular movement, shuffling steps, and stamping conform to African traditions of supplication, while by definition this activity is not recognized as a "dance."[22]

And although distinctions between shouting and dancing began to appear as the conversion of slaves to Christianity progressed, the emphasis on expressive movement in worship either superceded or coexisted with secular dancing, and served many of the same functions. Dena Epstein remarks that an account of an early nineteenth-century South Carolina plantation dance, a "jig" to fiddle music, with its "'shuffling, edging along by some unseen exertion of the feet from one side to the other' sounds remarkably like the descriptions of 'shouts,' religious dances from the same general area, as described during and immediately after the Civil War. The possibility that the African jig was the secular equivalent of the sacred dance, the 'shout,' deserves consideration and investigation."[23] In African practice there had been no need to distinguish between dancing and movement in service of religion. In Bolden even today, some of the shouts and shout songs have worldly or secular content, and the shouters speak of nonreligious ring plays (dancelike, nonreligious circle games) being performed at shouts.[24]

Still, the growing power of orthodox religion had the effect of suppressing secular dancing to musical instruments among the slaves on coastal plantations, just as it was doing, with varied degrees of success, among blacks and whites throughout the South. Epstein considers Sir Charles Lyell's 1845 account of a "holy dance" on James Hamilton Couper's plantation in McIntosh County, Georgia, to be the first description of the shout: "Of dancing and music the Negroes are passionately fond. On the Hopeton plantation above twenty violins have been silenced by the Methodist [Baptist?] missionaries. . . . At the Methodist prayer meetings, they are permitted to move round rapidly in a ring, in which manoevre, I am told, they sometimes contrive to serve as a substitute for the dance, it being, in fact, a kind of spiritual *boulanger*. . . ."[25]

Epstein commented that "Sir Charles received the impression that there was a direct connection between the ban of secular dancing and the development of the shout, as it came to be called. Other visitors were never told this, or connected the shout with African ritual."[26] It would seem that the two assumptions about the origin of the slave shout are not mutually exclusive: the call-and-response singing and the percussion that were part of the shout (though they were not described by Lyell) are derived from African tradition and not from European-influenced jig dancing to the music of fiddles; though the "holy dance" clearly became more important as a form of community emotional outlet and expression after secular dancing had been banned.

Epstein gives "fragmentary references to some kind of sacred dance, not always identifiable as a shout from the 1840s and 1850s,"[27] but she cites one condescending account by a Methodist minister in Maryland in which "two details identify the true shout: it took place after, not during, a church service, and it was a ring dance. Following the close of the prayer-meeting. At a given signal of the leader, the men will take off their jackets, hang up their hats, and tie turbans, and the company will then form a circle around the singer and jump and bawl to their heart's content."[28] Epstein has found the "earliest known use of the term 'shout'" in an account by an unidentified Englishman of a conversation with a Beaufort, South Carolina, Episcopal minister in 1860:

> "Heathenish! quite heathenish! . . . Did you ever see a shout . . . ?"
> I responded in the negative, and inquired what it was. "Oh, a dance
> of negro men and women to the accompaniment of their own voices.
> It's of no particular figure, and they sing to no particular tune, impro-
> vising both at pleasure, and keeping it up for an hour together. I'll defy
> you to look at it without thinking of Ashantee or Dahomey; it's so sug-
> gestive of aboriginal Africa."
> I had the opportunity, subsequently, of witnessing the perfor-
> mance in question, and can indorse the lazy gentleman's assertion.[29]

Disparaging as this description is, it is correct in identifying the shout as essentially West African. There is one other report of an antebellum shout from Georgia, written some time after the fact by Georgia Bryan Conrad, a Georgia woman describing ring shouts performed by her family's slaves. It confirms that the term "shout" was in use in the pre–Civil War period. Unlike the unidentified Englishman's account given above, Conrad was genuinely appreciative of the practice, which she perceived as something of an endurance contest; she was also the first of several commentators who recognized the "modern cake-walk" or the minstrel show "walk-around" as decadent secular offshoots of the plantation ring shout:

> When we were at our summer house in Glynn we always attended the servants meetings, which generally took place in the afternoon on Sunday, and Saturday, and Sunday nights. The afternoon performance we always attended, lingering at the door of the house until we were invited to enter and take seats, which consisted of rough benches placed around the wall. How we envied those who took part in the active shouting and singing! With what bated breath we watched the constant movements, the circling around and around, the bending, the scraping, wondering which of our favorites would hold out the longest! The modern cake-walk is a travesty upon the old-time shouting Negro. One is an affectation; the other, the spontaneous outburst of a naturally religious spirit.[30]

Possibly some of the reason for Conrad's admiring if somewhat condescending attitude toward her family's "servants" in the praise house was because of the fact that her reminiscences were published by the Hampton Institute, which was dedicated to the "improvement" of rural southern blacks. Roger Abrahams has recognized that the slave corn shucking ceremony, a circle dance akin to the ring shout, was encouraged as a display performance by the masters who "saw it as an entertainment verging on the spectacular." However, the slaves saw it as celebration and "came to recognize in the obligatory play and performance an opportunity for cultural invention and social commentary."[31]

Stuckey cites an early report by Fredrika Bremer of a camp meeting in Macon, Georgia, in 1850, at which black and white preachers preached simultaneously to their respective races; the blacks in attendance numbered three thousand, and Stuckey considers the setting to have been "favorable to African values." Bremer described fervid religious activity in tents, where singing, along with "gongs and rattles" and the beating of hands and fists upon the worshipers' chests, was accompanied by a woman moving in a counterclockwise circle with a sacrificial goat under her arm.[32]

There have been reports of the practice of the shout in inland regions and John and Alan Lomax recorded a shout as far west as Louisiana in 1934.[33] Sterling Stuckey considered the shout ubiquitous in nineteenth-century African American practice. The shout, or what has been described as the ring shout, has taken many forms; nonetheless, what we might call the "classic" ring shout—characterized by its separation from formal worship, its use of a separate band of singers, basers, and percussion players, its body of "shout songs" (usually) separate from other hymns and spirituals—was most widely practiced in the coastal areas of Georgia and South Carolina, especially on the barrier islands and adjacent mainland areas where, it is generally agreed, there was the greatest degree of retention of African practices in slave culture. On the plantations of this region rice was grown on land near the water and salt marsh, and its cultivation required backbreaking labor in the construction of drainage systems; large numbers of slaves also were employed in the cultivation of Sea Island cotton, the other principal crop in the sandy ground adjoining the salt marshes. Typically the average number of slaves per owner in the coastal Beaufort district of South Carolina "in 1860 was twice as great as the average for the state as a whole."[34] This large slave population, the strong African-derived culture, and the success of the missionary movement in suppressing secular music and dancing all coalesced in making the ring shout a widely practiced if not totally accepted form of expression by the time of the Civil War.

On November 7, 1861, the Union fleet overcame the Confederate defenses of Port Royal Sound, and the sound and surrounding South Carolina Sea Islands remained in Federal possession for the rest of the Civil War. All local whites immediately fled,[35] and during the ensuing period of the "Port Royal experiment" when the occupying northerners set about to instruct (and in the process learn about) the freed slaves, the ring shout and other slave traditions were observed and reported in far greater depth than before. Epstein gives a full account of the work of such observers as Thomas Wentworth Higginson, Unitarian minister and colonel of a black regiment of freed South Carolina slaves; he was also the author of *Army Life in a Black Regiment*. Epstein's work also discusses the first serious collectors of slave songs and authors of the unprecedented collection *Slave Songs of the United States* (1867), William Francis Allen, Charles Pickard Ware, and Lucy McKim Garrison; she characterizes Allen as "a trained historian and philologist, Ware a student fresh out of Harvard when he went to South Carolina . . . [and] Garrison . . . the only practicing musician among the Northerners who collected slave songs in the Sea Islands during the Civil War."[36]

According to Epstein, "descriptions of the shout written before the Civil War were perfunctory and vague . . . [while] the Northerners who partici- pated in the Port Royal experiment were fascinated by what was to them the most exotic practice of the freedmen for which they were unable to get any clear explanation. The more conventional found the practice shocking, sacreligious, and perhaps a bit frightening . . . [but many] were curious and admiring."[37] It is necessary here to reprint some of the descriptions cited by Epstein because they provide a richer picture of the shout traditions, and the response of outsiders to it, than anything written later in the nineteenth century and indeed up to the twentieth-century descriptions by collectors Robert W. Gordon and Lydia Parrish. These descriptions are important as documentation of the striking similarity of the shout as practiced in Port Royal in the 1860s to the tradition surviving today in McIntosh County, Georgia.

While most of the 1860s accounts of the shout refer to the kind of shuffling step still practiced today by the McIntosh Shouters, Higginson de- scribed a variety of steps in a diary entry of December 3, 1862:

from a neighboring campfire comes one of those strange concerts half powwow, half prayer meeting. . . . These fires are often enclosed in a sort of little booth made neatly of palm leaves covered in at the top, a native African hut in short; this at times is crammed with men singing at the top of their voices—often the John Brown song was sung, but oftener these incomprehensible negro methodist, meaningless, monot- onous, endless chants with obscure syllables recurring constantly & slight variations interwoven, all accompanied with a regular drumming of the feet & clapping of the hands, like castinets; then the excitement spreads, outside the enclosure men begin to quiver & dance, others join, a circle forms, winding monotonously round some one in the cen- tre. Some heel & toe tumultuously, others merely tremble & stagger on, others stoop & rise, others whirl, others caper sidewise all keep steadily circling like dervishes, outsiders applaud especial strokes of skill, my approach only enlivens the scene, the circle enlarges, louder grows the singing about Jesus & heaven, & the ceaseless drumming & clapping go steadily on. At last seems to come a snap and the spell breaks amid general sighs & laughter. And this not rarely but night after night.[38]

Today's shouters stress conscious control; they do not mix the kind of whirling and staggering that Higginson describes, which they would refer to as "falling out" and which usually occurs in response to some element of church worship rather than in the more formalized ring shout. Nonetheless, like Higginson's troops, they value the skillful display of performance ability and like that group are interested in gaining approbation both from within their fellow shouters and from outsiders. Up to the present, participants in the tradition appreciate varying degrees of skill among the shouters. It is worth quoting at length William Francis Allen's diary entry describing a Christmas shout at his school in 1863.

Billy [a freedman] came to Mary [Mrs. Allen] and asked if she wouldn't like to have a "shout" so forthwith the tree was shoved into a corner and the floor cleared. This "shout" is a peculiar custom of these people. . . . Mr. Eustis told me to-day that so far as he knew (and he is a native of South Carolina) it is not only peculiar to these islands, but to some plantations. Perhaps it is of African origin, with Christianity engrafted upon it just as it was upon the ancient Roman ritual. At any rate, it arises from that same strange connection between dancing and religious worship which was so frequent among the ancients and which we find in the dervishes, shakers, etc. These people are very strict about dancing, but will keep up the shout all night. It has a religious significance, and apparently a very sincere one, but it is evidently their recreation—just as prayer meetings are the only recreation of some people in the North. They do not have shouts very often, and were very glad to [have] the excuse to have one in a large open room. We went to see their regular Christmas shout in Peg's house last night. They had a praise meeting first. . . . At last they cleared the room and began, and a strange sight it was. . . . On one side of the room is a table, and in front of it stood young Paris [Simmons], Billy and Henry, who served as *band.* Billy sang, or rather chanted, and the others "based" him as they say, while . . . [six dancers] moved round the room in a circle in a sort of shuffle. This is the shout. Some moved the feet backward and forward alternately, but the best shouters—and Jimmy, I was told to-day, "is a great shouter," keep the feet on the floor and work themselves along over the floor by moving them right and left. It seemed tremendous work for them . . . and I saw the most skillful ones moved very easily and quietly. The shouters seldom sing or make any noise except with their feet, but work their bodies more or less; while the singers clap their hands and stamp the right foot in time. [Three others] sat or stood about and joined in the "base." When they had shouted in this way for several minutes, they stopped and walked slowly while Billy sang a sort of recitative interlude; then, when he began a new tune, they started off again. And their shouting varied a little according to the tune. In some they kept along with scarcely any change, and in others they would half stop, with a jerk at every change in the tune, and shift the foot in advance from right to left or left to right. Presently Billy joined the shouters, and Henry led the singing. . . . Today I was very glad to see the shouting again, to understand it a little better and catch the words. First there was a circle of the young people. . . . Church members are sometimes unwilling to shout with outsiders . . . I caught some of the words, which are evidently original.

"Jesus call and I must go—I cannot stay behin' my Lord," while the base sang "I must go." Another was "Pray a little longer, Jericho do worry me," while the base was "O Lord, yes my Lord." In singing this Billy sang very fast, "Jericho, Jericho, Jericho, etc." while the shouting was very rapid and excited. Another "Bell do ring,—want to go to meeting; bell do ring, wan' to go to shoutin',"—base "bell do ring" and here he sang in the same way "heaven bell" so fast that it sounded like "humbell—a—humbell—a—etc." These two were very fascinating. Another was minor, "Jesus died," and the singer repeated "died, died, died, etc." as he did "Jericho," only slowly and mournfully. Altogether it was one of the strangest and most interesting things I ever saw.[39]

This appreciative description is notable for its immediacy and perceptiveness; it is hard to imagine the field notes of a modern trained folklorist conveying more detailed information about performance and context. His speculation that the shout is "of African origin, with Christianity engrafted upon it" is certainly the case. Allen named several of the participants and regarded them as individuals with special abilities and functions. The detailed account clearly reveals similarities with the ring shout as it survives today in Bolden. The urgent singing, with its chanting call-and-response interplay of leader and answering singers continues much as it was described by Allen;

the term "basers" for the singers responding antiphonally to the leader, reported by Allen for the first time, is still in use today. Today's shouters leave most of the singing as well as percussion to the group off to the side and vary their steps and bodily movement according to the song, again just as Allen recorded. In connection with another early description of the shout, Sterling Stuckey commented that "hand clappers standing aside serve the role of drummers in Africa or Suriname."[40] The jerking "half stop" that struck Allen is used today in "Kneebone Bend" and is described by Lawrence McKiver as a "ketch-it," a technique he decries as unfortunately declining in practice. This feature also was described by Henry George Spaulding, a Unitarian minister who visited the Sea Islands in 1863: "At the end of each stanza of the song the dancers stop short with a slight stamp on the last note, and then, putting the other foot forward, proceed through the next verse."[41] Foot-tapping and clapping are still essential to the rhythmic accompaniment to the shout; the beat of the stick (apparently a substitute for drum beating) is the only integral part of present-day shouting in McIntosh County that is absent from Allen's description, as it is from all other reports of the shout from South Carolina.

Allen first published a description of the shout in an 1865 article concentrating on the "negro dialect" of the Sea Islands in the *New York Nation;* he calls the shout "the most peculiar institution of these people." He again mentions the "shuffling dance" in a circle and the accompanying singers who "base" the leader. "The 'base' almost always overlaps the tune, striking in before the line is finished, when the singer at once stops without completing the line, taking up his part again in his time before the base is quite through. The whole is accompanied by clapping of hands."[42] Allen again mentions "Bell da Ring," commenting that it is "a great favorite for 'shouting' and is also used for rowing . . ."; he cites several other specific songs used for shouting, including "Turn, sinner turn O!," which he calls "the most beautiful and dramatic of the shouts."[43]

The most detailed discussion of the shout, along with the printing of text and tunes of several shout songs collected by Allen, Ware, and Garrison appeared in their 1867 book *Slave Songs of the United States.* The book was innovative not only in that the introduction provided descriptions of the context of the songs and analysis of style of performance, but also in that the "editors provided musical settings for each of their 136 texts and variants, no small feat when one considers that Allen, Ware, and Garrison had no prior models to go by nor the benefit of tape recorders."[44] Though Allen acknowledges the difficulty of taking down music "from the lips of the colored people themselves" with "absolute correctness," he asserts, however, that "there are no mistakes of importance." He does recognize that paper and print will at best

> convey but a faint shadow of the original. The voices of the colored people have a peculiar quality that nothing can imitate; and the intonations and delicate variations of even one singer cannot be reproduced on paper. And I despair of conveying any notion of the effect of a number singing together, especially in a complicated shout. . . . There is no singing in parts, as we understand it, and yet no two appear to be singing the same thing . . . [this effect is called heterophony by modern musicologists]. When the "base" begins, the leader often stops, leaving the rest of his words to be guessed at, or it may be that they are taken up by one of the other singers. And the "basers" themselves seem to follow their own whims, beginning when they please and leaving off when they please, striking an octave above or below (in case they have pitched the tune too low or too high), or hitting some other note that chords, so as to produce the effect of a marvellous complication and variety, and yet with the most perfect time, and rarely with any discord.[45]

However inadequate as complete descriptions they may be, the tunes transcribed in *Slave Songs* are an invaluable record and will be referred to comparatively in the discussion of the shout songs still in use.

Allen begins his discussion of the shout in *Slave Songs* with a description reprinted from an article in the *New York Nation:*

> The true "shout" takes place on Sundays or on "praise"-nights through the week and either in the praise-house or in some cabin in which a regular religious meeting has been held. After prayers and hymns which are "deaconed," or lined out from a book with "wailing cadences" which are "indescribably melancholy," the benches are pushed back to the wall when the formal meeting is over, and old and young men, grotesquely half-clad field-hands—the women generally with gay handkerchiefs twisted about their heads and with short skirts—boys with tattered shirts and men's trousers, young girls barefooted, all stand up in the middle of the floor, and when the "sperichil"

is struck up, begin first walking and by-and-by shuffling round, one after the other, in a ring. The foot is hardly taken from the floor, and the progression is mainly due to a jerking, hitching motion, which agitates the entire shouter, and soon brings out streams of perspiration. Sometimes they dance silently, sometimes as they shuffle they sing the chorus of the spiritual, and sometimes the song itself is also sung by the dancers. But more frequently a band, composed of some of the best singers and of tired shouters, stand at the side of the room to "base" the others, singing the body of the song and clapping their hands together or on the knees. Song and dance are alike extremely energetic, and often, when the shout lasts into the middle of the night, the monotonous thud, thud of the feet prevents sleep within half a mile of the praise-house.[46]

Allen continues:

In the form here described, the "shout" is probably confined to South Carolina and the States south of it. It appears to be found in Florida, but not in North Carolina or Virginia. It is, however, an interesting fact that the term "shouting" is used in Virginia in reference to a peculiar motion of the body not wholly unlike the Carolina shouting. . . . Dancing in the usual way is regarded with great horror by the people of Port Royal, but they enter with infinite zest into the movements of the "shout." It has its connoisseurs, too. "Jimmy great shouter," I was told [this refers to Allen's diary entry of December 25, 1863]; and Jimmy himself remarked to me, as he looked patronizingly on a ring of young people, "Dese yere worry deyseff—we don't worry weseff." And indeed, although the perspiration streamed copiously down his shiny face, he shuffled round the circle with great ease and grace.[47]

As in Allen's day, today's shouters willingly express critical appraisals of other shouters' skill and bearing. Lawrence McKiver considered his aunt, Fannie Ann Evans, "the greatest shouter I ever seen." When I asked why she was greater than the others, he responded:

She was so active, you know, she had a lot of flesh, pretty good flesh on her. Aw, she was just the best I ever seen. If you would be able to see her, they would be singing this song, "going down heaven, easy walk, going down heaven, take my time" and she could be just as level, just the same as little trouble to her. Her meats'd be shaking, but she could be—so level in time. That's how they love to do—it's just like dancing, you know, some people dance jigging and jigging, others dance level. And she was the greatest shouter I ever seen in my life.[48]

The quality that Allen observed and that McKiver values has been described by Robert Farris Thompson as "coolness," in Africa a "strong intellectual attitude, affecting incredibly diverse provinces of artistic happening, yet leavened with humor and a sense of play. . . ." According to one of Thompson's informants, "it cools the town when you dance . . . when you finish . . . you are restored to repose." Thompson sees this attitude carried into African American dance and street comportment as "looking smart." He comments that it "is interesting that what remains a spiritual principle in some parts of Africa and the rare African-influenced portions of the modern U.S.A., such as tidewater Georgia, becomes in the mainline Afro-American urban culture an element of contemporary street behavior: 'Negro boys . . . have a "cool" way of walking in which the upper trunk and pelvis rock fore and aft while the head remains stable with the eyes looking straight ahead.'"[49] This movement and attitude is close to the "rock" motion in the shout "Move, Daniel" as performed today; perhaps this is why young children in the Bolden community have some success in imitating shouter Catherine Campbell's "rock" movement.

Allen reported that shouting "may be to any tune, and perhaps all the Port Royal hymns here [in *Slave Songs*] are occasionally used for this purpose; so that our cook's classification into 'sperichils' and 'runnin' sperichils' (shouts) . . . will hardly hold in strictness." Allen cites seven St. Helena hymns that "would rarely, if ever, be used for shouting; while probably on each plantation there is a special set in common use. . . . The shouting step varied with the tune; one could hardly dance with the same spirit to 'Turn, sinner' or 'My body rock "long fever,"' as to 'Rock o' Jubilee,' or 'O Jerusalem, early in de morning.'"[50] And that such a spiritual as "Nobody Knows the Trouble I Sees," familiar in later concert settings as a first-person plaintive song, was reported to have been used—by children—for the shout.[51] Today's shouters do not employ the term "running spirituals"; their term is "shout songs" and there is no overlapping of these with spirituals, hymns, or gospel songs.

In contrast to Allen's sympathetic accounts of the shout, other observers in the Port Royal area were disparaging or disapproving. Laura Towne's description of a shout in 1862 is similar to others, but she concluded, in a letter to her family, "I never saw anything so savage. They call it a religious ceremony, but it seems more like a regular frolic to me, and instead of attending to the shout, the better persons go to the 'Praise House.'"[52] Abolitionist Reuben Tomlinson considered it an unfortunate result of servitude, "the most ludicrous & at the same time the most pitiful sight I ever witnessed."[53] And teacher Harriet Ware allowed her pupils to have a Christmas shout in 1865: "I let the children sing some of their own songs in a genuine, shouting style, a sight too funny in the little things, but sad and disagreeable to me in the grown people, who make it a religious act."[54] Charlotte Forten, a northern black woman who taught the freedmen in the Sea Islands, also contrasted the shouting of children and adults in an article in *Atlantic Monthly,* characterizing the shouting of children as "comical," that of grown people "rather solomn and impressive than otherwise."[55] Charles Joyner notes that Forten "gradually came under the spell of the shouts, eventually even pronouncing them 'grand' and 'inspiring.' 'There is an old blind man, Maurice,' she wrote in her journal, 'who has a truly wonderful voice, so strong and clear,—it rings out like a trumpet. One song, "Gabriel Blow the Trumpet" was the grandest thing I have yet heard. And with what fire and enthusiasm the old blind man led off. He seemed inspired.'"[56]

Though she was impressed with such performances, Forten was at a loss to explain the meaning of the shout. Others who were negative in their reactions may have suppressed a realization that amidst the obvious biblical references in the songs and the strangeness of the shout itself there lay a protest against servitude and an affirmation of human spirit. The most sensitive observers, who were also the most liberal-minded, saw in the slave songs—spirituals as well as shout songs—an expression of both "'crushed hopes, keen sorrow, and a dull daily misery,'" balanced by "'words [that] breathe a trusting faith in rest for the future.'"[57] In 1861 abolitionists cited the slave spiritual "Let My People Go" as more than only a biblical statement, but also "a chorus that seems every hour to ring like a warning note in the ear of despotism";[58] the song was published in sheet music form later that year. And when the more perceptive observers inquired into the means of composition of the slave songs, they discovered song-making to be a vehicle of protest. Allen noted Higginson's discovery of "a poet" in action in the person of a young oarsman, whom he observed "raising" a song by decrying "de nigger-driver." Allen went on to cite James Miller McKim's account of how "new" songs were coming into being: "I asked one of these blacks—one of the most intelligent of them [Prince Rivers, Sgt. 1st Reg. S.C.V.] where they got these songs. 'Dey make 'em, sah.' 'How do they make them?' After a pause, evidently casting about for an explanation, he said: 'I'll tell you, it's dis way. My master call me up, and order me a short peck of corn and a hundred lash. My friends see it, and is sorry for me. When dey come to de praise-meeting dat night dey sing about it. Some's very good singers and know how; and dey work it in—work it in, you know, till they get it right; and dat's de way.' "[59] This sounds strikingly like Lawrence McKiver's way of describing the making of shout songs, even to the repetition of a key phrase like "work it in, work it in." While the meaning of such lines as "No more driver's lash for me" (*Slave Songs,* no. 64) is clear enough, deeper meanings encoded within many slave songs have been revealed only recently by McKiver and the other shouters of Bolden and will be considered later.

None of the early descriptions from South Carolina mentions the use of drums in connection with the shout. Drums generally were prohibited by slave owners in North America; drumming was considered pagan, and furthermore, drums might signal slave revolts from one plantation to another. In coastal Georgia, however, an African drumming tradition persisted. WPA interviewers met former slave Wallace Quarterman (b. 1844) of Darien in McIntosh County who recalled the use of drums in shouts and funerals on Skidaway Island near Savannah during pre-Emancipation times. "We sho did hab big time goin tuh church in doze days. Not many uh deze Nigguhs kin shout tuhday duh way us could den. Yuh needs a drum fuh shoutin. . . . We beat a drum at duh church and we beat a drum on duh way tuh duh grabeyahd tuh bury um." Quarterman went on to describe making "drums out uh sheep hide. . . . Some makes it out uh holluh lawgs wid skin obuh duh en an some ub um is as long as tree feet."[60] Katie Brown of Sapelo Island in McIntosh County was the granddaughter of Belai Mohomet, Thomas Spalding's Mohammedan slave driver. She told the WPA interviewers, "I dunno bout drums at churches. Use tuh hab um long time ago, but not now on duh ilun,—leas I ain heah um. Hahves time wuz time fuh drums. Den dey hab big times. Wen hahves in, dey hab big gadderin. Dey beat drum, rattle dry goad wid seed inum, an beat big flat tin plates. Dey shout and moob roun in succle an look lak mahch goin tuh heabm. Hahves festival, dey call it."[61] Apparently the beating of the stick came into use at some time as a substitute for drumming on the Georgia coast. The shouters of McIntosh County consider it an essential element of the shout tradition, and it was practiced on St. Simons Island as well: "The phrase 'Shout, believer, shout!' [in "Move, Daniel"]—accompanied by . . . [the] beating [of] a broomstick held vertically and pounded on the floor—comes at a faster tempo and signals the beginning of the shout step, which is then used throughout the ceremonial."[62] This confirms Lydia Parrish's statement that "on St. Simons they [for the shout "Eve and Adam"] always call for a broom handle, which, when knocked on the floor, provides an extemporaneous tom-tom. In McIntosh County, however, they are so proficient in tapping out the rhythm with their heels that they can dispense with both sticks and hand clapping. With their hands free, they are able to do things descriptive of the text which less skillful groups would not be at liberty to attempt."[63] We do not know which shouters in McIntosh County Parrish encountered. The shouters of Bolden invariably employ a broom or stick; a group of lead singer and basers provide hand and foot rhythms, and the stick beater allows the shouters in the ring to enact the elaborate pantomine to which Parrish refers.

In the mid-nineteenth century, the plantation shout was beginning to influence the greater American popular culture through the same institution that popularized the slave banjo (also of African origin)—that institution was the minstrel show. Early twentieth-century music writer Henry Edward Krehbiel recognized that a "secular parody of [the shout] can easily be recalled by all persons who remember the old-fashioned minstrel shows, for it was perpetuated in the so-called 'walk-around' of those entertainments. 'Dixie,' which became the war-song of the Southrons [*sic*] during the War of the Rebellion, was written by Dan Emmett as a 'walk-around' for Bryant's Minstrels in 1859."[64] The cakewalk might be, as Georgia Conrad observed earlier, another secular amusement that probably derives in some way from the ring shout; at the very least it stems from parallel "worldly" dance traditions.

Accounts of the ring shout are fewer in the years after the Civil War; one report was that made by William Wells Brown of an 1880 shout in a Nashville, Tennessee, church, performed by women who were incited to movement by the minister.[65] We do know that various forms of the shout persisted after slavery in coastal regions and beyond; perhaps it was so widely practiced that it was no longer considered noteworthy by most southern whites or outsiders. There is also the possibility that the ring shout, especially in the Southeast, was less visible to outsiders because of its frequent association with semi-secret societies functioning apart from official church structures, which did, nonetheless, greatly influence church affairs. Stuckey quotes Edward Channing Gannett, who observed the ring shout in Port Royal during the mid-1860s: "The evidence [Gannett] presents makes it clear that they grafted African institutions onto the Baptist church they attended: 'Subsidiary to the church are local "societies," to which "raw souls" are admitted after they have proved the reality of their "striving."'"[66]

While the southeastern ring shout persisted among Baptist groups, a related tradition, the Singing and Praying Bands, was well established among black Methodists in the Upper South and Mid-Atlantic regions. Jonathan David, who has documented the ongoing tradition of these "bands" in the Chesapeake Bay area, traces the origin of the bands from the period of the Great Awakening: "Camp meetings . . . proved to be fertile territory for the creation of a vast corpus of spiritual choruses. . . . Further, camp meetings, then as today, often ended with a grand march around the encampment, accompanied by singing. It was to these phenomena—the spiritual chorus singing and the grand march—that African converts brought pre-existing dance and song traditions in a process of syncretization."[67] David likens these marches to the shouts noted by such observers as Higginson, who had called the songs accompanying them "Negro-Methodist chants"; yet the forms that evolved further north, and the terms used by the participants, differed from those of the southeastern ring shout. According to David, "With the conversion to Christianity . . . the idea of religious 'dance' did become stigmatized; African worshippers in the Chesapeake region responded by calling this aspect of the shouting service a 'march,' and they generally discouraged crossing feet or lifting feet."[68] These modifications of African practice were not enough to convince such important black Methodist clergy as A.M.E. bishop Daniel Alexander Payne that the bands were not among the "bad customs of worship" that he opposed for decades. Payne, later to become the United States' first black college president through his position as first president of Wilberforce University, encountered the bands in Baltimore in the 1840s and again in Pennsylvania in the 1870s. In his memoirs Payne gave this account of his active opposition to the Singing and Praying Bands in this latter time:

About this time I attended a "bush meeting," where I went to please the pastor whose circuit I was visiting. After the sermon they formed a ring, and with coats off sung, clapped their hands and stamped their feet in a most ridiculous and heathenish way. I requested the pastor to go and stop their dancing. At his request they stopped their dancing and clappng of hands, but remained singing and rocking their bodies to and fro. This they did for about fifteen minutes. I then went, and taking their leader by the arm requested him to desist and sit down and sing in a rational manner. I told him also that it was a heathenish way to worship and disgraceful to themselves, the race, and the Christian name. In that instance they broke up their ring; but would not sit down, and walked sullenly away. After the sermon in the afternoon, having another opportunity of speaking alone to this young leader of the singing and clapping ring, he said: "Sinners won't get converted unless there is a ring." Said I: "You might sing till you fell down dead, and nothing but the Spirit of God and the word of God can convert sinners." He replied, "The Spirit of God works upon people in different ways. At camp-meeting there must be a ring here, a ring there, a ring over yonder, or sinners will not get converted."[69]

Payne noted in his journal some of the folk verses (which he not inaccurately called "corn-field ditties") sung by what were also termed "Fist and Hell Worshipers":

Ashes to ashes, dust to dust
If God won't have us, the devil must.

I was way over there where the coffin fell
I heard that sinner as he screamed in hell.[70]

Prayer, albeit in a form excoriated by Payne, was and still is an integral part of the singing and praying band practice, as was, from the testimony of the young leader, conversion. Conversion and prayer, as understood in Christian belief, are, by contrast, not a part of the ring shout as it has survived in Bolden, though an internalized form of supplication and summoning of life energies, and a feeling of the participant's being with the "Spirit," most definitely are. In contemporary practice in the Chesapeake Bay region, David describes a service where a band, under the leadership of a "captain," moves in a progression from prayers and hymn singing, to singing accompanied by some participants "elaborately miming the episodes described in the words they collectively sing"; then there is a shoutlike counterclockwise march around the mourners' bench and beyond, called "marching around Jericho." David notes that this refers to the celebration of the victory of the Israelites who "marched around the walls of Jericho when Joshua said: "Shout; for the Lord has given you the city" (Joshua 6:16).[71] David concludes: "The circular worship culminating in a march may be of African derivation, but the disciplined, social solidarity that it celebrates was also adaptive, and even crucial to survival for many Africans in America."[72] In this respect, despite differences in form, the singing and praying band service is similar to the ring shout as it survives in Bolden. Michael Schlesinger, who recorded the present-day bands with Jonathan David, recently told the author that the participants do not refer to their circular marches and processionals as "shouts" or "shouting," despite the fact that, as David established, the term "shout" is pivotal in the biblical text that is enacted in the bands' "march around Jericho."

In their singing the present-day bands as documented by David seem to have abandoned the "corn-field ditties" or shout songs of folk composition in favor of hymns and spirituals derived from hymns, along with improvised sung prayer. Payne's abhorrence of folk-style songs as well as his rejection of "heathenish" dancing (shouting) was probably shared by most highly educated members of the black clergy in the late nineteenth and early twentieth centuries. At the same time, the traditional Negro spirituals, through the performances of such polished groups as the Fisk Jubilee Singers, were gaining acclaim as an art form. The poet James Weldon Johnson valued and collected the spirituals, yet he disparaged the ring shout. Still, his description, probably the third written account of the shout by an African American (after Charlotte Forten and Bishop Payne), provides a vivid picture of the ring shout as he remembered it from his youth in Florida:

> Brief mention must be made of another class of Negro songs. This is a
> remnant of songs allied to the Spirituals but which cannot be strictly
> classified with them. They are the "shout songs." These songs are not
> true spirituals nor even truly religious; in fact, they are not actually
> songs. They might be termed quasi-religious or semi-barbaric music.
> They once were used, and still are in a far less degree, in religious

gatherings, but neither musically nor in the manner of their use do they fall in the category of the Spirituals. The term "shout songs" has no reference to the loud, jubilant Spirituals, which are so termed by writers on Negro music; it has reference to the songs, or, better, the chants used to accompany the "ring shout." The "ring shout," in truth, is nothing more than the survival of a primitive African dance, which in quite an understandable way attached itself in the early days to the Negro's Christian worship. I can remember seeing this dance many times when I was a boy. A space is cleared by moving the benches, and the men and women arrange themselves, generally alternately, in a ring, their bodies quite close. The music starts and the ring begins to move. Around it goes, at first slowly, then with quickening pace. Around and around it moves on shuffling feet that do not leave the floor, one foot beating with the heel a decided accent in two-four time. The music is supplemented by the clapping of hands. As the ring goes around it begins to take on signs of frenzy. The music, starting, per- haps with a Spiritual, becomes a wild, monotonous chant. The same musical phrase is repeated over and over one, two, three, four, five hours. The words become a repetition of an in-coherent cry. The very monotony of sound and motion produces an ecstatic state. Women, screaming, fall to the ground prone and quivering. Men, exhausted, drop out of the shout. But the ring closes up and moves around and around. I remember, too, that even then the "ring shout" was looked upon as a very questionable form of worship. It was distinctly frowned upon by a great many colored people. Indeed, I do not recall ever see- ing a "ring shout" except *after* the regular services. Almost whispered invitations would go around, "Stay after church; there's going to be a 'ring shout.'" The more educated ministers and members, as fast as they were able to brave the primitive element in the churches, placed a ban on the "ring shout."[73]

As we have seen, the shout has taken many forms. That described by Johnson seems to more closely resemble the shout reported by Higginson, with its repetitious chants and trance-inducing movement, than it does the shouts described by Allen, these being characterized by more formalized movement and rich vocalizing and rhythmic complexity, in large part provided by a separate band of singers and percussion makers. We have already noted that the form of the shout described by Allen closely parallels that of the present-day shouters of Bolden. The more demonstrative forms of shouting may be rooted in the fervor of the Great Awakening as much as they are in African practice, and these forms were very likely sources for the styles of worship in sanctified congregations in more recent times.

Johnson seems to associate the term "shout" with vocalization, while realizing that the shout involved movement. He does not describe a separate band of singers, nor does Robert W. Gordon, in his discussion of the shout in *Low Country Spirituals.* By the 1920s, when Gordon, a pioneering modern folklorist, did his field work in the Sea Islands, the ring shout had become one of several forms of the shout in practice. Gordon describes these in detail, but always refers to the shouter and singer as the same individual:

> Quite as varied in form as the spiritual, and frequently accompanying it, was the "shout" or religious dance. . . . Not all spirituals were shouted. But whenever spirituals were sung they demanded a certain rhythmic movement of the body . . . to shout properly . . . it seems to have demanded that the singers be standing if not actually taking steps. . . .
>
> . . . One of the simplest forms, known as the "ring shout" is apparently widespread. In this, the shouters form a circle and proceed around and around in a sort of slow processional, facing in one direction. The speed is determined by the particular song they are singing, but the advance is always slow and dignified. Hands are held in front, palms together—sometimes vertically at the height of the breast, sometimes horizontally and a little lower—and clapped with a single or double beat. The body sways at the hips, and dips as the knees bend. The feet shuffle, each step advancing the body slightly.
>
> . . . Even in this simple type of shout, several different steps may be used. In two cases of the ring shout, both collected in one locality, I found a marked difference between the ways in which the verses and the chorus were shouted. The ring was formed as usual but the singers walked slowly while they sang the verse:
>
> Oh we'll walk around the fountain,
> Oh we'll walk around the fountain,

Yes we'll walk around the fountain—
Oh religion so sweet.

The shuffling steps in much quicker rhythm began only when they
came to what we should normally call the chorus:

Oh religion, oh religion, oh religion so sweet!
Oh religion, oh religion, oh religion so sweet!

These lines were repeated again and again without pause for perhaps
ten minutes; then once more the singers dropped back for a single
verse to the walk; then shuffled again to the same many times repeated
chorus. On asking more about this peculiar type, I was informed that
it was known as a "walk around." The words themselves may have
been responsible for the introduction of the walk. One wonders if this
religious walk around might possibly be the relic of a very old type,
and perhaps the ancestor of a later walk around as performed by the
blackface minstrels on the stage.

    . . . Shouting took many other forms. One might shout acceptably
while standing in one place, the feet either shuffling, or rocking backward and forward, tapping alternatedly with heel and toe, the knees
bending, body swaying, and the hands clapping. Or a singer could alternately advance and retreat. Not infrequently two singers would
shout facing one another in a sort of competition of skill or endurance.
Sometimes this was done with great dignity and grace, but not infrequently one of the singers, in an attempt to outdo the other, would
introduce body motions that seemed to have very little to do with
religion. Occasionally one of the women would throw her hands
high above her head and pivot slowly, or would indulge in steps that
seemed to carry with them a reminiscence of more formal dancing
seen at one of the balls at the big house. The line between shouting
and dancing was strictly held. Shouting could be indulged in only
while singing a spiritual. Under no circumstances might the feet be
crossed. These two rules were universal and inflexible. In addition, the
older and stricter church members held that the foot should never be
entirely lifted from the floor. Beyond this it was a matter of discretion.
It was universally agreed that shouting was dignified, that it was a worship of the Lord, and that certain motions were not fitting. For example, whenever, in my own experience, one of the younger women—

perhaps while singing the spiritual "Rock, Daniel, rock! Rock I tell you, rock!" where the body rocked from side to side—placed her hands on her hips, elbows out, and "danced kimbo," or when she showed the slightest tendency to move her feet too far apart, or to cross them, one of the older sisters would reprimand her sharply, often quoting the words of the spiritual—"Watch out, sister, how you walk on the cross! Yer foot might slip an' yer soul got los'."[74]

Gordon goes on to note that the shout played a role in social life outside the church, as a "favorite form of diversion in the cabins. On holidays, celebrations, or weddings, and particularly on Watch Night, it was a regular custom."[75] He gives two examples of shouts that "even showed tendencies toward becoming a game. Acting out the story was not infrequent. 'Rock, Daniel,' shows a trace of this. A better example might be chosen in 'Where is Adam?'"[76] Both of these shouts are still performed in this way in McIntosh, though "Going down to the mire," Gordon's third example of a shout bordering on a ring play, is not.

Gordon perceptively recognized that the shout had a social as well as religious function, and he clearly understood the continual interchanges in African American folklore between secular and religious forms when he confirmed earlier, and less expert, observers' likening of the ring shout to the plantation walk around. Roger Abrahams has noted that "the ring shout [and] the buck and wing, among others, [had been introduced in the nineteenth century] as popular dance forms."[77] In the early twentieth century, the ring shout was understood to be seminal to another secular art form, jazz. Rudi Blesh and Harriet Janis maintain that as late as the 1950s, the ring shout was "still danced in some of the churches of Harlem, the most sophisticated of all American Negro Communities," and they connected it to early jazz through their interview with the Harlem pianist Willie "the Lion" Smith, who told them: "Shouts are stride piano—when James P. [Johnson] and Fats [Waller] and I would get a romp-down shout going, that was playing rocky, just like the Baptist people sing. You don't just play a chord to that—you got to move it, and the piano-players do the same thing in the churches, and there's ragtime in the preaching. Want to see a ring-shout? Go out to the Convent Avenue Baptist Church any Sunday."[78] Though one is inclined to trust the insights of an artist like Smith when he likens musical elements in worship services to rhythms of stride piano (in his essay concluding this book, musicologist Johann Buis discusses the 3 + 3 + 2 rhythm that moves from African patterns into jazz), Harlem churchgoers might not have been as ready to compare their forms of worship to jazz. Of course, neither the piano, nor any other musical instrument besides body percussion and drums or such drum substitutes as the broomstick, was used in nineteenth-century religious shouts, but the acceptance of pianos and other instruments into northern sanctified churches by Smith's time certainly facilitated the use of the same or very similar musical forms being put to sacred or worldly use. Interestingly one of Smith's fellow musicians, the famous pianist James P. Johnson, remembered secular dancing, complete with musical instruments, from his childhood in New Brunswick, New Jersey, at the end of the nineteenth century; and he described this as the "ring-shout." As he told Blesh and Janis: "The Northern towns had a hold-over of the old Southern customs. I'd wake up as a child and hear an old-fashioned ring-shout going on downstairs. Somebody would be playing a guitar or jew's harp or maybe a mandolin, and the dancing went to *The Spider and the Bed Bug Had a Good Time* or *Susie, Susie.* They danced around in a shuffle and then they would shove a man or a woman out into the center and clap hands. This would go on all night and I would fall asleep sitting at the top of the stairs in the dark."[79] The circular shuffle certainly invites comparison with the ring shout as it had been described many times; yet the use of instruments and the secular songs associate this practice with the plantation or minstrel show walk around. Johnson may have been casual about his use of the term "ring-shout"; he seems to have blurred the distinctions between religious shouts and secular forms, claiming that much of his music was "based on set, cotillion, and other southern dance steps and rhythms."[80] Yet one of his most famous compositions, "Carolina Shout," was intended to evoke many forms of early African American music and dance and was a mainstay of Chicago rent parties; it was the piece on which Duke Ellington, Cliff Jackson, and Joe Turner cut their musical teeth.[81]

Apart from its influence on secular forms, the shout had become an essential element of sanctified worship by the twentieth century. Stuckey argues that the sanctified church was a "harborer of the shout"; he cites folklorist and anthropologist Zora Neale Hurston's statement that "'shouting' is nothing more than a continuation of the African 'Possession' by the gods . . . [and is] still prevalent in most Negro protestant churches and is universal in Sanctified churches."[82] The singing and percussion produced by feet, hands, drums, and tambourines in sanctified services is certainly a direct outgrowth of the slave shout. Many call-and-response songs sung by sanctified congregations and twentieth-century gospel quartets and choirs clearly flow from, and structurally are similar to, early shout songs sung by the shouters of Bolden; it would require little more than up-to-date rearranging to adapt such a shout song as "Blow, Gabriel" to modern gospel performance style. Body movements in sanctified churches, characterized by groups of singers and worshippers swaying to music and individuals "falling out" and moving with the Spirit, differ from the formalized movement of the southeastern ring shout. Yet James Baldwin's fictionalized description of a Harlem sanctified church service, also cited by Stuckey as evidence that the shout was embedded in the practice of that church, bears a striking resemblance to the Bolden shouters' "eagle wing" in "Move, Daniel": "While John watched, the Power struck someone, a man or woman; they cried out, a long wordless crying, and, arms outstretched like wings, they began the Shout."[83]

In the early twentieth century, the shout was evolving into myriad forms of African American worship and was influencing such modern secular musical genres as jazz. (Jazz was an unusual survival of an African form of the shout, employing distinct African language and dance forms with the latter resembling the coastal ring shout.) The shout was described in an inland region:

> Near Calhoun, Ala., there are Africans who came to this country after the Civil War. The leader in their "shout" will hold his right hand to his face, his head bend to the right, and call out, "Higha!" the circle rejoining:
>
>> Leader: Higha!
>> Circle: Malagalujasay!
>> Leader: Higha!
>> Circle: Lajasaychumbo!
>> Um! Um! Um!
>> Leader: Higha!
>> Circle: Haykeekeedayo, ho!
>
> The women move slowly around the circle, the left foot somewhat in advance of the right, the right drawn up to the left as it is moved on a few inches at a time and in rhythm. The body is slightly bent, with the buttocks protruding. The men stand erect.[84]

In the mid-1930s scholarly attention was turned to the shout by an article in the *Bulletin of the Folk-Song Society of the Northeast;* its editor, the eminent folk song scholar Phillips Barry, stated in the article that the shout is "wrongly thought to be a Negro product. . . ."[85] Barry was aware of mid-nineteenth-century accounts of the "sacred dance of the Negroes," and elsewhere he cited an account of freed blacks settled in Brownsville, Maine, who at the "prayer meeting in their homes . . . joined hands and circled around the room, singing and cracking their knuckles at regular intervals, and shouting fervent exhortations and prayers."[86] Barry cites several Old Testament references to shouting as vocalizations, including Ps. 47:1: "'O clap your hands, all ye people, shout unto God with the voice of triumph.'" He concludes: "Since American Protestant Christians, white and black, sought precedent for doctrine and ritual in the English text of the King James version, we doubt not that the *shout,* with the accompanying *patting* or clapping of hands, was in part a conscious effort sincerely to reproduce a kind of worship having unimpeachable Scriptural authority."[87] He asserts that Robert Gordon's "view that the name has nothing to do with shouting . . ." (cf. Gordon, *New York Times Magazine,* April 24, 1927) is refuted by the earliest descriptions of the shout. Barry quotes one such description in which the understandable confusion of shout as movement and the English word for vocalization occurs: "'They go around in a circle, singing, shuffling, jerking, shouting louder and louder' (F. Moore, *Rebellion Record* 7, pp. 21–22, from a Port Royal Correspondent)." Of course at that time, Alonso Dow Turner had not yet published his finding that the Afro-Arabic word *saut* (sometimes pronounced "shout"), which describes a religious dance, had become part of the Gullah dialect.[88] Barry, who was so scrupulous in using field observation and information from his ballad-singing informants in the Northeast to reinforce his scholarship, should have given greater credence to his colleague's position, for Robert Gordon must have been told unequivocally by blacks that vocalizations were one thing and shouting was another. Barry, along with George Pullen Jackson, was part of a scholarly revisionism of that day seeking to correct what they perceived as a mistaken belief that black spirituals flowed directly from Africa by showing precedents for spirituals in white hymnody. Challenging one of Gordon's examples of a "very old Negro shout" utilizing call-and-response, Barry asserts that "if such is the typical form of the shout, the whites had it first," and he refers to a published camp meeting song from 1844.[89] This begs the question of African call-and-response to say the least, as well as the African characteristics of the overlapping leader and chorus lines, and the recognizably African stylistic traits of the holy dance itself. Barry attempts to demonstrate English derivation of the circle dance by showing "a Negro shout *Round About the Mountain* . . . [which] is unmistakably based on the [Anglo-American] ring-play *Go round and round the Valley*."[90] Yet Barry's source for the former, Henry Edward Krehbiel, does not identify it as a shout (song) but rather a funeral hymn sung by a Kentucky ex-slave.[91] Another argument of Barry's is that "a [black] singer such as Sojourner Truth, who is known to have been under Shaker and Millerite influences . . . would sing camp-meeting hymns as she heard Shakers and Millerites sing them. . . ."[92] Barry also points out that the Shakers had a circular "walk-around" and "shuffle," while their singing was demonstrably British. Barry's points do not demonstrate that the shout and accompanying songs are not, in large part, of African origin, but rather that European Americans also had call-and-response singing and circle dances, and that the two traditions coincided and might have reinforced each other.

By the late 1920s, the shout was reported as occurring "infrequently" on St. Helena Island, South Carolina, by T. J. Woofter, Jr., who remarked that in the shouts he observed a "step . . . much like that which gained world fame as 'The Charleston.'" He also describes a march in church as the collection was taken, where "marchers shuffle and sway to the music . . . the procession looks somewhat like a country dance. One or two old women sway in their seats and finally stand up and shuffle as if they are about to break into a 'shout.'"[93] By the late 1950s, when Guy Carawan documented traditional culture in the Carolina Sea Islands, the ring shout had died out there. However, a form of the shout in which singers set up call-and-response patterns to shout songs while moving and creating polyrhythmic clapping and stamping in place was practiced during a Christmas Eve all-night service at Moving Star Hall on Johns Island, South Carolina:

A woman with a thick rich low alto started off in the corner and very soon was joined by some deep resonant male "base" from another corner. The falsetto wails and moans sailed in to float on high over the lead. By the time the whole group of about sixty worshippers had joined in, each freely improvising in his own way, the hall was rocking and swaying. . . . All sorts of overlapping sounds wove and blended together to produce a breathtaking whole full of rough beauty. . . .

. . . From the moment the watch started with the first song, heads and bodies began to sway, feet began to tap, and hands to clap in time to the singing. They sang with their whole bodies. These motions increased in abandonment as the evening went along until finally the "shouting" started. Someone stood and started rocking back and forth doing a special rhythmic step and hand clap in time to the singing. Others followed and by the end of the song the whole group was on its feet singing, dancing, and clapping in a joyous noise to the Lord. . . . Three different rhythms were being carried by the hands, feet, and voice.[94]

Guy Carawan has contrasted the shouting style of the Johns Island singers with that of the Georgia Sea Island Singers, commenting that the two groups have been together on many occasions.

Both their singing styles and the rhythm and motor behavior of their shouting styles are quite distinct. The Georgia Sea Island Singers use a fuller harmony with a distinct bass line; the Johns Island sound is much more stark, with harmonies in thirds, fourths, and fifths, and there is no bass line. . . .

One year at the Newport Folk Festival, the Moving Star Hall singers were on stage doing a number of songs in their particular shouting style. A group of West Africans, the Ashangi Dancers, were sitting near us in the audience. They said that, in their culture, there was a particular name for the rhythm of the Johns Island shout. They were excited by the thought that this rhythm had been brought to the United States and had survived in a contemporary form.[95]

This anecdote may confirm that the Johns Island shout is a distinct African-derived performance mode rather than a later development of the shout, without the circular motion of the ring shout. We might add that the McIntosh style of singing shout songs employs harmonic intervals less frequently than the Johns Island group to the north or the St. Simons Georgia Sea Island Singers to the south.

In inland areas where the ring shout has been forgotten, the term "shout" is used today to refer to a worshiper who "falls out"—is possessed by the spirit and stamps, gesticulates wildly, trembles, and makes rapid steps in place. We have seen this frequently in Baptist and Holiness churches, and movement rather than vocalization is always understood as shouting, although the shouter may make exclamations. Charles Perdue located a description of a "ring shout" in a paper entitled "Negro Folklore," presumably from Georgia in the 1930s, but the practice described is clearly the other meaning of shouting: "Now Dinah jumps into the aisle rolling from side to side in ecstatic abandon, shouting:

> You kin hol' my bonnet,
> You kin hol' my shawl,
> I'm shoutin' in de cool,
> Thank Gowd!"[96]

In 1994 a black church invited those tuned to an Athens, Georgia, gospel radio station to attend a service and to "wear your shouting shoes." The term endures in countless spiritual and gospel song texts—"shout on my child," "shout together children, don't get weary," and of course, "shout all over God's heaven."

Lydia Parrish distinguished between two types of shout, the ring shout and a shout in which "individuals are seen in church using the same rhythmic shout step."[97] The latter was clearly the form Carawan later observed. Parrish first saw the ring shout "at the hall of the Queen of the South Society on St. Simons Island. . . . Hard board benches were an unimportant matter. Little had I suspected, when Margaret took care of my room at the Arnold House years before, that she could outdo the Ouled Nail Dancers, of Biskra—if she wished. As it was, she wiggled her hips shamelessly, held her shoulders stiff—at the same time thrusting them forward—kept her feet flat on the floor, and, with the usual rhythmic heel-tapping, progressed with real style around the circle—goodness knows how."[98] This is typical of Parrish's combination of condescension toward and perceptive admiration of the culture she recorded—at once signaling the servant status of a black woman of St. Simons and prudishly commenting on what must have been her "rock" movement in the shout, yet appreciating the artistry of the performance, and describing it with an eye for detail. Parrish observed the shout on St. Simons and collected shout songs not only there but in the counties to the north along the Georgia coast, including McIntosh. She devoted an entire chapter of *Slave Songs of the Georgia Sea Islands* to "Afro-American Shout Songs," and encouraged the perpetuation of the shout and other traditions through the performing group she organized, first called the Spiritual Singers of Georgia. According to Alan Lomax who first visited St. Simons with Zora Neale Hurston in 1935 and returned to record traditional songs and shouts in 1959, "each member received a button which distinguished him as a 'Star Chorister' and signified that he was a folk singer and dancer in the great tradition of the region. This group was led by the older people who constantly instructed the members in the oldest and finest style of singing and dancing. The chorus performed for visitors and tourists who had by then begun to stream onto St. Simons."[99] This group became the Georgia Sea Island Singers, who continued to reenact the ring shout for the public after it had died out in community practice on St. Simons. Frankie Quimby of the present Georgia Sea Island Singers believes that the last "house to house" community shouts took place on St. Simons in the late 1930s, but confirms that the tradition was kept alive through performances for tourists at local plantation-museums and luxury hotels, such as the Cloisters on Sea Island; she added that the St. Simons group was augmented at times by shouters from Camden County to the south and McIntosh to the north along the coast.[100] This may have brought about some exchange of reper- toire and encouragement of the shouting practice during the 1940s and 1950s, though the shouters of Bolden maintain that no shouters from McIn- tosh County went to St. Simons to shout during that period. In recent de- cades such collectors as Alan Lomax and Guy Carawan have viewed surviv- als of slave folk-song and shout traditions in a positive light as being among the cultural forces that help sustain coastal African American communities. On the other hand, folklorist Bruce Jackson was convinced that Parrish had gathered remnants of "historical folklore" out of a misguided nostalgia for a bygone social order: "Folklore is a dynamic thing. . . . Though historical folk- lore is of historical interest and present importance (so we may better un- derstand the present), it is nevertheless of only collateral current interest— unless our interest is sentimental only."[101] We have noted negative attitudes toward slave folk-song traditions from orthodox white clergy as well as black and the scorn of the shout even from such a figure as James Weldon John- son. It is interesting to see the wish to marginalize survivals of slave folk- song culture coming from a modern academic folklorist advocating a "dy- namic" rather than antiquarian approach to folklore. Of course, at the time in which he wrote, Jackson was aware of continuing coastal slave song traditions mainly in the context of stage performances by the Georgia Sea Island Singers, who had been organized for preservationist purposes by Parrish, though he must have been aware of the continuing South Carolina musical traditions documented by Guy Carawan. Yet, by the 1960s one could not be blamed for assuming that slave songs (except some spirituals) were no longer actively being sung, and that the ring shout in community practice was extinct. This was also the conclusion of Mary Arnold Twining, a fieldworker who worked extensively on the Georgia and South Carolina coasts in the early 1970s: "Although it is within the memory culture of the South Carolinian Sea Islanders, they no longer do the actual 'ring shout' dance. The Georgia Sea Island Singers perform it in concert situations but the religious-social context has long since been lost." [102]

Meanwhile blacks in McIntosh County were continuing to sustain a slave-song and ring shout tradition for reasons of their own that were far from sentimental in an ongoing, though changing, community context. The shout there is taken very seriously as it is understood as a way, besides serving God, of honoring the ancestors who had endured slavery. Lawrence McKiver says, "We're proud of what we're doing 'cause it come from our poor parents." Deacon James Cook, born in 1886, said, "I found them [among others, his slave-born father, Nathan Cook] doing it when I got old enough to realize anything about the shout. . . . In those days they were so loving of each other after the service they would move the benches in the prayer-house and shout. . . . We are still holding to that yesterday tradition that was taught by our fathers and mothers . . . that brought it from our homeland in Africa. They knowed how to shout, they loved to shout—that was one of the ways they gave thanks to God. . . . Someday we'll be shouting the harvest home." [103]

Lawrence McKiver and Shouters at the McIntosh County Shouters' First Public Performance,
St. Simons Island, Georgia, 1980

Deacon James Cook at the National Folk Festival, Wolf Trap Farm, Virginia, 1981

"Pickin' Up Leaves," McIntosh County Shouters at the National Folk Festival,
Wolf Trap Farm, Virginia, 1981

Andrew "Bo" Palmer (with broom), Lawrence McKiver, and the shouters at
the National Folk Festival, Wolf Trap Farm, Virginia, 1981

McIntosh County Shouters at Filming Session, 1985

Watch Night Shout in Bolden II, 1982

Mt. Calvary Baptist Church and Annex, Bolden

Lawrence McKiver, Sea Island Festival, St. Simons Island, Georgia, 1983

Learning to Beat the Stick I, Watch Night 1992

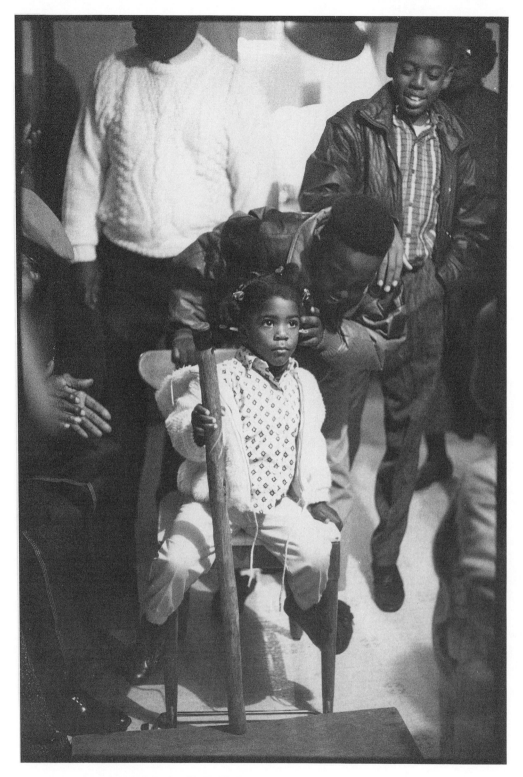

Learning to Beat the Stick II, Watch Night 1992

Lawrence McKiver on His Porch, 1993

The McIntosh County Shouters, 1992. Back row (from left to right): Catherine Campbell, Carletha Sullivan, Elizabeth Temple, Thelma Ellison, Vertie McIver, Doretha Skipper; front row (from left to right): Odessa Young, Lawrence McKiver, Benjamin "Jerry" Reed, Oneitha Ellison.

"Pickin' Up Leaves," McIntosh County Shouters at the Morton Theatre, Athens, Georgia, 1994

McIntosh County Shouters at the Black Arts Festival, Piedmont Park, Atlanta, Georgia, 1994

McIntosh County Shouters Performing the Ring Shout, Black Arts Festival, Piedmont Park, Atlanta, Georgia, 1994

Rev. Nathan Palmer, Bolden, 1993

The McIntosh County Shouters, 1994. Back row (from left to right): Freddie Palmer, Harold Evans, Lawrence McKiver; front row (from left to right): Odessa Young, Carletha Sullivan, Venus McIver, Vertie McIver, Thelma Ellison; and in front, Benjamin "Jerry" Reed.

2 "One Family of People"

The Shouters of Bolden

The McIntosh County climate was very demanding. Hot, humid summers and the rice fields and tidal marshes made for a perfect combination for the breeding of mosquitoes. Many slaves died from disease and the attrition created by the constant nuisances of mosquitoes, sandgnats, alligators, and poisonous snakes. Most of the planters spent only several months during the colder months on their plantations. The rest of the time, they fled to other places—Savannah, Charleston, New York, Philadelphia.

The Civil War brought an end to all this, of course.

—Buddy Sullivan, *Early Days on the Georgia Tidewater*

[Hinesville developer] Clay Sikes won County Commission zoning approval Tuesday for a 141-acre mixed residential and commercial development at the South Newport interchange on Interstate 95. Sikes said he wants to build a historical theme park that simulates the old colonial town of Sunbury, complete with cobblestone streets and clipper ships in an artificial lagoon. "History is not something you can buy, but it's certainly something you can sell," he said.

—*Darien News,* Febuary 10, 1994

The shouters of Bolden live mostly within walking distance of each other, on land they own—land where their grandparents and great-grandparents were slaves. The community is also known as "Briar Patch," after the Briar Patch cemetery. "The Wyllys had a slave [plantation] and the Hopkins had a slave [plantation] and . . . the Hopkins' slave [plantation] was further away in the section they call Meridian. See, the grave yard sorta briary over that side, so that give it the name of Briar Patch," Lawrence McKiver told us.[1] He had this information from the previous generation: "You found some of them old folks, they remember what section of the slave they was into."[2] The Hopkins plantation, called Belleville, was one of the great rice plantations of McIntosh County on the eve of the Civil War. Though its owner, Charles Hopkins, outspokenly opposed secession, Belleville was "partially destroyed during the Federal naval raid up the Sapelo River in November 1862."[3] The Wylly plantation was known as the Forest. "On the Sapelo River about 1½ miles east of present-day Eulonia, was one of the finest estates in McIntosh County during the antebellum period, being regarded for the quality of its cotton and produce."[4] Though Charles Hopkins sold Belleville to his son in 1877 and the Forest was still in the possession of Alexander William Wylly when he died there in 1872, much of the land of the two plantations was bought by freed blacks who had worked there as slaves. As Lawrence Mc-Kiver told it, "After the . . . old slave holders had lost their power, see he couldn't keep nobody down no more. He start selling off. That's how come we get this land. He start selling off his land around here—could buy acre land for a dollar, but how would you get that dollar? Getting that dollar at that time is as hard now for me to get a thousand dollar bill. You work so long before you get that dollar. You could buy a whole heap of land for five, six dollars, maybe three or four dollars at that time. Right now an acre land cost you twenty-five hundred dollars."[5]

Rev. Nathan Palmer told his niece Carletha Sullivan why land on nearby Sapelo Island was owned by blacks: "He said . . . because of mosquitos and different things, the white people they all got sick, so they had to move away, and the black people was the only ones could stand up under the insects and so forth, that's how they got to own Sapelo. He also told me that his mother's mother was here, in this county, and her husband was sold to a slave [plantation] in Jessup, in Wayne County. And when they were freed . . . their owners used to let them visit each other . . . the husband was coming here to her, and she was going to him, and they met somewhere in the middle, and they decided to come back here, and they settled [in] the piece of property that they really call the Briar Patch which we still own, and that's where they got together and settled."[6]

London and Amy Jenkins were the grandparents and great-grandparents of the shouters of Bolden, who have inherited from them a wealth of tradition and lore from slavery days, including the ring shout and the shout songs. When today's shouters recall the shouts of their youth when the "old sisters" moved impressively around the ring in their long dresses, they are speaking of blood sisters, Lizzie, Celia, Sarah, Nancy, Martha, Emmaline, and Charlotte, all daughters of London and Amy Jenkins; not much is remembered of the Jenkinses' two sons, Henry and Esau. Carletha Sullivan confirmed that "in fact . . . it all [the tradition] goes back to them because . . . all of the people in this area, for the exception of those that moved here, are their children. . . . When I was a girl, we were the only family of people in this entire community. But since we grew up here some of the younger ones met husbands and brought them in. But when I was a child, we were the only family of people in this entire area." Freddie Palmer agreed, "All of us was one family, one family of people."[7]

Carletha Sullivan and Freddie Palmer, cousins who are both in their middle years, are two of the third generation out of slavery to carry on the shout and the shout songs. Palmer is a paper mill worker. Sullivan has lived in Germany and New York and has worked in health care; her present job is driving imported automobiles off ships in the port of Brunswick. We were talking in the living room of Carletha's neat brick home in Bolden, a half mile up the road from Lawrence McKiver's house; on the wall are displayed photographs of Carletha's children who have earned university degrees. Carletha and Freddie credit the persistence of strong family ties in the community with the continuation of the shout tradition. Palmer said, "It had a lot to do with the tradition of that time of year. Everybody would look forward to going out there . . . go and do that shout. I remember our grandmother we [he and Carletha]—we had the same grandmother—taught us these things. Martha Palmer, oh boy, yeah, [she was] a singer and a shouter."

"All of 'em," Carletha added. "All the sisters. In fact, all the shouters are descendants of those sisters."

"The Jenkins family," Freddie Palmer continued, "my mother, Oneitha's [Ellison's] mother, Lawrence's mother, the Reeds, all of them were one family, from the Jenkins."

"Probably," said Carletha, "because our great-grandmother was a slave, and probably because all of her children, like I said [stayed] right in this community. . . . Some people moved, but all of those sisters . . ."

Freddie picked it up: "They stayed right here."

"They stayed, and some of their children stayed," Carletha continued. "So that's probably the reason why it held in this community. I guess you can tell by the dialect."[8]

Lawrence McKiver's mother, Charlotte Evans, was one of the daughters of London and Amy Jenkins. It was from her that Lawrence learned that some of their ancestors had come to Georgia by way of the Bahamas, which accounts for some speech intonations in the community even today that Lawrence characterizes as "Nassau-ified." And from his mother and his oldest aunt, who was born in slavery, he learned of the hardships of slavery: "I know one of my aunts back in the slave [slavery], the oldest aunt, she was sold to a slaveholder over in little place called Doctortown right away from Ludowici over there. Her name was Sister Celia. Used to call her Aunty Celia. . . . And she was over there for long time. Then some my mama people went over got her and bring her back to Ludowici, bring her on. It was really spoken Sunday before last in church—we have a big family reunion down there. And we bring her back here. And that how come we know her."

"So sometimes families would be split up that way," I said. "Be split up," Lawrence confirmed.

> See like when my mama tell me . . . like a bunch of family have maybe
> five or six boys or girls, healthy, big, strong, a slaveholder come in and
> this slaveholder he sell one just like you would sell a hog or a cow or
> something. He wanta buy one, he come here and he buy it, he take
> that one. Well I won't know where my sister goin' or I won't know
> where my brother goin'. He take 'em off. He didn't have no way to get
> back and keep that one. If I were to go into the other section, maybe I
> could be courtin' some my relatives, you know, you understand, it
> could be my sister. . . . So that's the reason she would tell us things like
> that what happen. It's a frightful thing sometimes to think about it, but
> it just happen that way, understand. People tell how hard they have to
> work sometime, they didn't have the right food, didn't have the right
> clothes. I walk to the woods out there now, I can show you ditches out
> there. We walk out there looking for our hogs and stuff, she say the

slaves dig this ditch. . . . I'm gonna even write a song, I'm trying to write a song this morning, I'm gonna write it about some of the wish, that I imagine some of the wish that my poor slave folks would say they want they children to see or come on down through. Or like I would want my children to see. Better days. I'm gonna write a song about it. I hope I live to get the song wrote.[9]

Old spirituals from slavery times were sung as work songs in the fields and down through Lawrence's time: "'I Won't Be a Slave No More.' I heard 'em sing, I was taught about the song . . . my mama and all them, they'd be working in the field, they'd be singing that stuff, I drift along with them . . ."

> Well I won' be a slave no mo',
> No I won' be a slave no mo',
> Befo' I be a slave I rather be buried in my grave,
> And go home to my Lord and be saved.

> Well I won't work another day,
> An' be treated this-a-way,
> Befo' I work another day,
> An' be treated this-a-way,
> Befo' I work another day, and be treated this-a-way
> I will be dead, and buried in my grave.

Lawrence related this song to the tradition of the Ibos who drowned themselves on St. Simons Island. "They tell me, twenty-seven, they link themselves together and walk on down to the sea, the slaves was speaking about, that chained themselves together, and walk overboard and drown, they had made up their mind that they wasn't gonna do it, just all link themselves . . . and walk on . . . gone out to the tide to sweep them away. They wasn't gonna be treated that way. . . . Some people always say, well, old Hopkins used to go fool the slave over, people say, come from this tribe of Africa, that tribe of Africa. . . . I'm gonna pay you good wages, come with me." Lawrence believes there is no way to know what tribe he is descended from. "Some people say West Africa, or South Africa, or North Africa, but they was hauling them from every which-a-way, any place they could get them, so my mama never told me what tribe. I think she got it about right, they coming, jus' like hogs come to corn." Lawrence did not recall the old folks using African words:[10] "No, not exactly. The old folks talk bad, jus' like I do. My mama wasn't a slave. My mama's mama was. My mama told me they was more like Nassau-ified people. She always would say that. From some kinda island. My daddy's side, they come from Carolina, me being mixed Nassau and Geechee. . . . Geechee, that's true! So therefore I'm in the midst of danger!" We both laughed at that. Lawrence calls his dialect, when he is asked to provide a name for it, "Geechee talk," saying that the term Gullah was not heard until applied by outsiders in recent times. "I didn't hear about no Gullah. They say Geechee. It's just a flat way of talking."[11]

Lawrence remembers his mother telling him old folktales from slavery times:

> Any time we have a long conversation talking about the black race and the white race, they would tell the old fun stories that my mother tell me her mother tell her. One time the slaves didn't have no meat, and they killed one of the old boss's cow, a small one, and they goin' to take all the intestins and throw 'em in the river. And the little boy whose name was Jack was out play' in the street, and the old lady was inside the little old kitchen cooking, and [the master] said, "Where's [your] daddy?" Little boy say, "Daddy went to throw away the cow guts." The old lady in the kitchen say, "Turn around, Jack!" He [the master] say, "What you say, boy?" He say, "Pa goin' to Cow-gut Creek." That's to keep the boss from knowing that he destroyed one of his cows. We'd sit around the table, and she'd tell them. I never will forget that.[12]

Another of the tales McKiver heard from his mother was of the fox and the rabbit, popularized by Joel Chandler Harris as the famous "Tar Baby" tale.

> Yeah, my mama done told me that story the fox caught the rabbit. All the time she always have something to tell her children. The fox catch the rabbit and, say, "Gonna eat you." The rabbit say, "Please don't eat me." Say, "That's all right." Say, "I know what I do with you." Say "I'm gonna find some way to get rid of you, you don't want me to eat you. I'm gonna throw you in the well." He say, "Aw, you throw me in this well, I get outta here and I be all right. Throw me in the well if you want." Say, "You gonna get out the well, I'm not gonna throw you in this well." "I get outta here and I be all right. Throw me in the well if

you want." Say, "You gonna get out the well, I'm not gonna throw you in this well." Say, "I know what do, I'm gonna cut your head off." Say, "I jump around and I get my head, I live again." Fox say, "I know what I do with you," say, "I'm take you and carry you to this big briar patch right here, see those thick thorns on it," say, "I'm gonna throw you in that bunch of thorns and they'll stick all in you and you can't get out." Rabbit say, "Please don't do that. You do that," say, "I'll die," say, "I can't live no longer. Don't throw me in that briar patch, please." Say, "That the very place I'm gonna throw you!" The fox grab him and throwed him in the briar patch. Say, "Thank God, thank God," say, "you put me right where my mama and my daddy raise me," and off he gone. We would laugh at that, you know.[13]

When we asked whether this animal story related to folks, McKiver first denied it, then reconsidered its meaning: "I never say it related to any folks, but I imagine some folks could fool you. You think sometime you hurt 'em and you just give 'em a pleasure, you know. So she would tell us stories like that. We would get a kick out it, you know, say the rabbit fool the fox." Another story that related specifically to slavery, was one of the "Massa and Old John" tales that McKiver heard from his mother.

She tell us a story one time, a old slave story. I just think about that this morning, laying up here in the bed. Said old John, me most has to leave and gone off. He got most a horse, he got on a horse and he ride over to the next plantation. He had a horse. Fellas didn't know who the horse belong to. He say master give that horse to him, but he had done stole master' horse and ride over there while master gone. He out there showing off. So they rented a house and they was sitting down in that house and the horse got sick and laid down. And so one fella come and say, "Who that horse belong to?" He say, "That horse belong to me." Say, "That horse down on the ground, kicking and can't get up." So John run out the house and look and see the horse down there sick. He knew that master' horse, he had stole it. So he say, "Help me get this horse up." Say, "Can't pick up the horse." John say, "Don't give a damn, help me get the horse on my shoulder, I take the horse on back." He want to carry the horse on back to the master. Say, "Help me get the horse on my shoulder." He was a big, strapping man.

He gonna take and tote the horse back to where master was to keep from getting beat. And I was thinking about that, think the whole morning long. We laugh, you know, he couldn't tote the horse. . . .[14]

Slaves had to live by their wits to survive the rigors of the system, and fear of the lash was constant. McKiver continued that, "eatin' dry food the biggest part of the time, no meat, you gonna do *something* to revive us. The slaves, they didn't have the education, but they was slick, you can find slick people without being educated now." McKiver returned to the hardships of slavery and the strategies of mutual support during slavery times and later, as recounted by his mother and aunts.

Oh, yeah, sometimes they get whipped. Some of them get so they couldn't work out their tasks, they got so much rows they have to work a day, and if their couldn't come to the specification, sometimes they get whipped. Sometimes the strong one got to go back and help the weak one, you know . . . maybe I say I don't want you to get a whipping I don't want the boss to get mad with you . . . when I get done my half, I'm stronger than you, I come back and help you. That's the way they tell they would do. And even up to *my* mother's time—modern times brings on a change. I can remember for myself, the black owned about twelve . . . miles, it's the biggest black plantation in the state of Georgia—and you know how they would do? They would get in the field with their hoe and help this one work *their* field—they swap work—and they go to the next one's field and work that out, and they go to the next one till they go around the whole plantation, and they work 'em all out. See, I help you and you help me and keep on like that as a gang, let's get together. And while things growing . . . a bunch of the ladies, they get together, they get them a scaffold just the length of a quilt . . . then they get them old cloths and they quilt, until they go all around like that. Then they take in the corn, take in the rice, take potato, put them in the cellar, we kill the hogs, stock would be back in the woods, everybody have *their* hog, have a mark on them—I know my hog from yours—kill up our hog, smoke 'em, put 'em in the smokehouse, and they be good, you can believe that, that old hickory smoke, you take a knife and cut you off a piece. And then we turn back around, get the cane . . . and everybody get their cane cut down, they start grinding cane for two or three weeks before Christmas, and they have candy pulling until coming up to the week to Christmas, to Christmas Eve, we shout the New Year in. In that shouting we go from house to house . . . and we have that coffee, them biscuits, tater pones, all different things . . . and that's the way this plantation used to be.[15]

Perhaps McKiver had lapsed into the first person as a rhetorical device in this narrative carrying the folkways of his community forward from slavery times; but it is more likely that he is remembering his own youth in the early part of this century as differing very little from the rough but cooperative agrarian existence that prevailed from slave times and sustained such traditions as the ring shout. The shout songs and the specific movements of the shout were continuing reminders of slavery, some more pointed than others. McKiver recalled one song that he used to hear, "Drive Ol' Joe." "Ol' Joe, he was a slave . . . he was the one that watch the workers, you know, if the workers didn't do good, he would tell the big boss. And they made them a song about that. After the slave [slavery] was over, Joe want to come along with 'em, but they didn't like Joe, they made a song:

Drive ol' Joe,
> Drive on, oh Lord, drive on,
Drive 'im out the window,
> Drive on, oh Lord, drive on,
He tried to kill us,
> Drive on . . .

And the song, while they're singing the song, they had, the sisters had a handkerchief, like they're driving, they don't want him around 'em, you see, they dislike him for what he done—already did."

"And they would explain to you what the song meant?" I asked.

"What the song meant. See, I don't know how they do it, but they could just make them up a song. My mother was a great songster. And I have about five more auntie sisters sing, and I have a sister, can sing—a mockingbird, they would just sing them songs. That's the way I get a chance to—I would just hang around them, I would just take heed of that, and I just followed it on down through. . . ."[16]

Two shout songs passed down to today's elder shouters from their slave grandparents through their parents dealt specifically with the freeing of the slaves, "Read 'em, John," and "Jubilee." The first was said to refer to a slave,

John, who had managed to learn to read a little in the days when this was forbidden to slaves, and he told his doubtful brothers and sisters that they indeed had been freed:

> One by one, two by two, three by three and fo' by fo',
> Tell all the members, read 'em, oh, read 'em and let me go!

"Jubilee" celebrated the Emancipation:

> Shout, my children, 'cause you're free,
> My God gave me liberty.

and referred bitterly to the masters' cynical use of religion as a means of controlling the slaves:

> Call me Sunday Christian
>   Oh, my Lord,
> Call me Monday devil,
>   Oh, Lord, Jubilee!

In the years after the Emancipation the churches in the Bolden community were tiny praise houses in the woods, just as they had been during slavery days; some of these praise houses persisted even as larger churches were becoming better established in the late nineteenth century. Lawrence McKiver described what he remembered of the old praise house in the settlement:

> Well, they would come out, where you see the church there, was a little thing, wasn't n'ar as big as my house to where the heater is [about fifteen feet in length], and they had a little old wood heater in the floor to keep them warm, they would walk out, there was no road like there is here now, they had them some fat light for splinter, they get to the pond, they light the splinter, they hold that up, they walk cross the pond on two logs, laid down side by side and a leader with a light and a leader behind with a light wood. Fire torch! They come across the pond, then they put out the splinter, and lay them down there. That's on a Tuesday night. Then they go to this little church, they had little old lights to the side, like a lantern. And they would get in there. And one man, Reverend Palmer's daddy, they call him Deacon Joseph Palmer, he was a good songster, and he could read more than any of

the rest of them, he would give out the hymn, and they would sing the hymn, this one would kneel down in prayer, and the other one would kneel down in prayer. They would say, "Lord, they always did believe there would be a better day," understand. It was in their mind, every one of them, that things didn't have to be—like it was. At that time. They would say, "Lord, help my children to see better days than what I'm seeing." They would say that word. I'll remember that until my re-memberance go. I can see in my mind's eye. I can see them old folks, when they get down in prayer, every one of them, they pray, but they would say that: "Lord, help my children to see better days than what I'm seeing." Those things, that's just something that would stay with me. And they would come back after the prayer service, Tuesday night, they would go back cross the log. Thursday night they come back again. They do the same thing. They sing old spiritual songs.

Then he [Deacon Joseph Palmer] say this, the Lord know his in-tention, he knowed them old folks' intention, keep on through, keep on through, and the shout have come up long time back, little old places, they shout round the community, in little old board houses, old sills underneath the floor, they shout till they break down that one! We have a two-weeks' stretch in there, understand, we go from house to house in the community, they cook them old cat-head biscuits, maybe they cooked their peas in the rice, old country food, "soul food," I call it, they eat and they shout, they eat and they shout, and if they break down this house, like you shout this evening and break it down the night before we go home, well tomorrow, before we start shouting again, we build our house back up! Fix it back up. Go to the next house. And we just keep up 'round the community. . . . Then Watch Night we goes to the [church] we shout two times there, we shout for Christ-mas Eve, and we shout for the New Year. Two nights we go to the church.[17]

The original praise house was "way back in the settlement . . . made out of logs, like a log cabin." This praise house was just like the praise houses of slavery days.

Back then, there wasn't no church. People used to walk from here to Darien, to the First African Baptist Church in Darien, that's the biggest black church in Darien. That's right there, sitting by the jail house now, the church is way over one hundred and some odd years old, way over, and the old folks used to walk way over to church then. After time move on, then Crescent have a church down there . . . a Baptist church, my old parents would go there, they tell me. They decided they would leave from there and start them a church over here, you see that big field, back over that hill, they had a little church over there. Then they moved from over there and they come right over here to where you see this [Mount Calvary] established over here. Started with a bush arbor, then they come on into a church. . . . They [had to] walk too far, and they start the next church. Prospect was the next church. Calvary branch off in this settlement. This settlement down there was over the Hopkins slave side. And this was the Wylly slave side. . . . Therefore, the people over here, they branch off from this church . . . they come back into Mount Calvary. Back over there . . . is the New Homes Baptist Church, and the other churches branch off and branch off and branch off. Churches more to the convenience of the settlement of the people.[18]

Odessa Young, one of the eldest of today's shouters, confirmed that even in slavery days Christmas was the main time for shouting: "They had to get the barn, the master say so, Christmas time—my mother told me those things, her mother told her, and her mother told her—and get the barn, clean that up, get everything so those two weeks, they have a good shout. That's the only time they had to shout. After that, was time to go back in the field, they had a taskmaster all their days." Odessa's conversation continued, typically for the shouters of Bolden, to flow seamlessly from what she was told about the slave shouts into her own early experiences in the shout, to the present day: "This was more of a prayer than anything else. We not supposed to cross our feet—that would be a dance. I was right there. And I can still shout. If they set that song right, and I get my blood sort of warm, I can shout. It make you feel good, you get something out of it. Praise the Lord, think where you come from."[19]

There were no shouts in the old praise house across the pond in Mc-Kiver's memory, nor did he hear of shouting there in earlier times. But shouts were held in the Mount Calvary church, after Christmas and at Watch Night prayer meetings, besides the shouts held in homes through the holiday season. Mount Calvary had been organized in the 1890s, and the original building, near where the present church stands, was the location of shouts McKiver recalls from his boyhood.

> We shout in there. Build a big log fire outside. They cook the biscuits, the old peas in the rice, with a hog jaw bone and ears and put that in the peas and rice, and eat, and drink coffee and biscuits, that's what we had. [We would shout] right in the church. We didn't have no annex, we didn't have none of that. It wasn't such a stylish thing as now. Lord, now, we don't want you to shout in the church on the carpets! It wasn't like that. It wasn't nothing but the old board floor, old rough boards, but they'd scrub it till it be so smooth and white, they clean that church, the floor be thick boards, and they shout in the church. They move the bench back, shout there in the church.[20]

Freddie Palmer recalls that then "Everybody had a song they would sing. You take my uncle, H. K. Jackson, he used to sing nothing but 'Blow, Gabriel.' I don't care—that's the only song he would sing . . . he had the voice, sort of easy voice, he would sing 'Blow, Gabriel,' and Sarah and all would sing up a storm." Palmer was born in 1942 and is one of the best of the younger songsters in the community. He patterns his singing after that of his uncle, Nathan Palmer, "Oh he could sing, that little man could have sung a song!"

Carletha Sullivan commented, "He can still sing. His voice is still just as strong."

Freddie also remembered the wood fire outside the church and recalled that "some be out in the churchyard doin' their little sipping." Inside, the old folks would sing and encourage him and the other youngsters to shout and sing.

> There used to be two benches, in church, where the deacons would sit. That time of year, the sisters would sit on the front seat, on New Year's Eve, after prayer meeting, one would sing one—each had a special song they would sing, and round and round they go all night like that. Then they get some of the mens that were good singers like Uncle Nathan, H. K. Jackson, those, they would sing. Each of them would sing a song. So wasn't much of a problem being there all night. . . .
> And they would always tell you, "Get up there and shout, we singin' our heart out and nobody don't want to shout. Get up on that floor. . . .

You can sing if you can't clap," they would say. And they would always encourage us like that.

Carletha Sullivan recalls that the old singers were "strong!"

Freddie Palmer agreed, "Strong, and they could do anything right, they could background."

Carletha said, "If you could have heard what they used to do, this we do is nothing."

"There would be more basers?" I asked.

"More everything. Goodness, they could make some noise."

"The only thing they didn't have the stick on the board floor," Freddie added.

"Did they ever tell you why they used the stick?"

"They used to use the broom," Carletha explained. "They probably started using the stick after they started going places [performing for the public, beginning 1980]. Because, all along, they used to go grab the broom . . . get the broom out the corner."

Freddie agreed, "They just grab a broom."

I asked, "I heard the stick was a substitute for drums. Did you ever hear anybody say that?"

Carletha said, "They could send a signal through drums. I remember when I was a girl, I don't know if Freddie remember or not, we used to live more that way, and they used to holler to each other through codes . . ." Freddie continued,

> They would holler. And even the ladies, when they would be going to work, they would signal each other. Just holler, tell 'em we ready. . . . They had strong voices, their voices just carried. I don't know why your voice don't carry like that now. But they could holler. My aunt and my mother used to go places together, they would walk. Aunt Thelma Ellison, she's my father's sister, and she would call her, holler, you know, signal she was ready, and they would meet down there. . . . Uncle Nathan used to call Adam, when they would meet to go fishing, they would just whoop, "aaa-hooo," and directly you see him coming through the woods with a sack, go across to the river, go fishing casting for mullet all night. That's their communication.[21]

Large-scale rice farming had died with the end of the slave system, but the ex-slaves and their descendants who owned and worked land in the

Bolden community had continued to get by with subsistence farming, growing a few cash crops, working for neighboring whites, and earning some living from the rivers and the sea. At the turn of the century Jim Cook, who lived in the neighboring Ardock community, was walking fifteen miles every day to Darien where he worked as a stevedore, stowing timber that had been rafted down the Altamaha River on schooners that would take the timber to England and Germany as well as ports up the Eastern Seaboard. Cook was the grandson of Ishmael Nephew (1760?–1838) who had been the bell ringer of the First African Baptist Church in Darien, of which he was probably a founder.[22] Cook sang a work chantey, related to the spiritual "Jacob's Ladder," that he remembered and sang with pride for the rest of his days.

> I'm a noble soldier (hah)
>> Soldier of the Jubilee
> I'm gettin' old and crippled in my knee,
>> Soldier of the Cross. (hah)
>
> Too young to marry!
>> Soldier of the Jubilee (hah)
> I'm gettin' old and crippled in my knee,
>> Soldier of the Cross. (hah)
>
> Do you think I'll make a soldier?
>> Soldier of the Jubilee (hah)
> I'm gettin' old and crippled in my knee,
>> Soldier of the Cross. (hah) [23]

Union Baptist Church in the Ardock community had a shout tradition, and Jim Cook told of looking forward to shouting the New Year in and beating the stick. He considered the shout to be, as well as a means of "praising the Lord," a "holy dance, more than the frolic," acknowledging its function as a physical outlet while making the nice distinction between dancing and shouting for the Lord.

Shouting was discontinued about forty years ago at Union Baptist Church, as well as at the New Homes Baptist Church. No one recalls when shouting ceased on Sapelo. People in neighboring communities knew that Mount Calvary was the place to go on Christmas and New Year's if they wanted to attend a shout, even those who had moved up north. Freddie Palmer affirmed, "Everybody would head to Calvary those two nights."

Carletha Sullivan agreed: "Far and near."

"From New York," Freddie continued. "Christmas Eve, New Year's Eve, Calvary was the place."[24] He remembers the nights of the shout as being a "big time"; Carletha recalls that those were the only nights of the year that children could stay up all night.

Although church was the center of organized worship and dancing was permitted for teenagers and adults while children amused themselves with circle games (ring plays), the shout was considered to be, in the words of Lawrence McKiver, "really the main entertainment in this community, and two more communities, the Crescent community and the New Homes community, they used to do the shout. But when time come on, move on, those people drift out from it, but the Bolden community, they say the 'Briar Patch,' never did drop it. 'Cause I had a sister, and a mama, and some aunties that could sing it, and then we had some more people that could shout it, and we kept it right here."[25]

Hearing these repeated testimonials to the inspiration and instruction in the ring shout of the preceding generation, and of the importance of the tradition as a seasonal celebration, we are approaching an understanding of why it has endured through the twentieth century in Bolden. The shout, functioning outside of organized church practice, demands a sizeable, cohesive, and dedicated group of participants in the tradition—this has been provided by the descendants of London and Amy Jenkins. Traditional African American church practices require a leader (the pastor) who can and often does come from outside the immediate community; individual expression and worship through prayer and solo singing, and group worship through congregational singing and liturgy, are commonly practiced in black Baptist, Methodist, and sanctified churches throughout the South. Preachers, worshipers, and choirs visit nearby or distant churches and can immediately participate. But, at least in this century, the ring shout has become dependent on special received knowledge of songs, the shout movements, and a shared understanding of its history. A few people in a community were not enough to keep the shout going. "When our church was rebuilding, we didn't have an annex, we would go to old man Jim Cook's church in Ardock," McKiver recounted. "We spend the Watch Night down there with them, we did that for several years, we get our annex built, we didn't go back down there anymore, we spent our Watch Night in our own church. They didn't have the singers that we got . . . we got more singers than they have. They had one man and a lady that could sing a little shout song a little bit, but they couldn't touch us. My mother died in '79. When my mother died, I was sharing Watch Night with the Cooks." The new church, built around 1950, had a cement floor, "But you cannot do much shouting on a cement floor, nothing qualifies for the shout, so we spent it down there. After they built the annex, we moved back home."[26]

McKiver does not remember when the shout was discontinued at New Homes but said, "We would go over and try to swap shout with them for a while, but they got so they didn't have anybody to be interested in it, we had only one shouter [Vertie McIver] out of New Homes. . . . She was married to my brother, she come over to this community, and she wanted to belong to us in the shout, so we took her in."[27]

Physical isolation is often presumed to be a factor in the survival of early folk traditions. One thinks of the Gaelic singers of the Outer Hebrides or the Appalachian mountaineers from whom Cecil Sharpe collected ballads early in this century. Notions of isolation frequently are tinged with a romantic disregard for the dynamic of change within folk communities and of communication and contact with other regions and social classes that exist within many of the most supposedly cut-off groups. In the case of the Sea Islands, it frequently is assumed that early and African-derived traditions survived more strongly on the "isolated" barrier islands than in nearby mainland areas. Even in earlier times this was not necessarily the case; in South Carolina slaves on the islands often had easier contact by boat with urban centers, such as Charleston, than did their cousins on the mainland. But most important in the sustaining of old traditional practices is community cohesiveness and sufficient economic support for community survival, particularly with regard to such a tradition as the ring shout, that requires, as we have shown, a relatively large group steeped in the tradition. In inland rural areas in Georgia, the demise of cotton-farming because of the boll weevil and the Great Depression decimated communities and caused large-scale emigration to the North. In Bolden, members of the community owned their land and could grow subsistence crops; they could not be evicted as could sharecroppers elsewhere. Being near the rivers and sea provided employment even during hard times. "Oh, there was always something to do," Carletha Sullivan told us.

"Oysters in the winter time, shrimp . . . in the summer, and crab is in the summer," added Freddie Palmer.

Carletha continued, "There was always work, you were right on the water. In fact, I think that's probably how we got here, 'cause we were right on the water." We laughed. "Seriously! They would come to all those little islands. And Sapelo was a stop off."

Such men as Lawrence McKiver were commercial fishermen, and women went to work at Cedar Point to shuck oysters. "Shuck oysters, walk there cold in the morning, walk back in the evening when they get through," recalled Carletha. Later the women in the community got a van and went as a group to seafood packing plants, such as Pledgor Packing in Darien and Quik-Freeze in Brunswick. The easy access to Interstate 95 made it possible to drive to work yet continue to live in the home community. Freddie Palmer currently works in a paper plant in Savannah, up the interstate.[28] Savannah is a forty-five minute drive up the coast from McIntosh County; Brunswick, to the south, is even closer. Though there has been some emigration, difficult living conditions, and an increase of crime and drug use, Bolden, on the mainland, continues to be a viable community. In contrast, on nearby Sapelo Island, accessible only by boat, the black population base dwindles year by year.[29] And on St. Simons, as on some of the Carolina Sea Islands, tourism, real estate development, and higher taxes are driving away even many poorer blacks who own their land.

Bettye Ector provided some insights as to why the ring shout has persisted in Bolden:

> Well, part of the reason why the tradition goes on, the older people in this community help carry the tradition on. You have several older people who are very active in the community, even though they are ninety-plus, still in the church, you know that they're there, they're not sedentary. You find the high school drop-out rate on Sapelo is very low, most of the kids from Sapelo finish high school, but as soon as they finish high school, they leave. They may not migrate any farther than Brunswick, but they leave, and here, you don't see that. They very seldom leave from the community. . . . They maintain homes and families here in the community. They have a sense of home. They don't stray very far away.[30]

Ownership of land, economic viability, strong family and church ties all have worked to sustain the community and enabled the continuation of the shout; the influence of such elder tradition bearers as Nathan Palmer,

Lawrence McKiver, and Odessa Young has been noted by Bettye Ector. Respected in church and community, they have prestige and effectiveness in the practice of the shout itself. Their leadership in the practice is effected in an important way through the mechanism of call-and-response as it functions in the singing of the shout songs and the "setting" of the shout for the shouters. Call-and-response is a feature of most, though not all of the shout songs, and is a powerful force for forging group and community cohesiveness while reaffirming the authority of the leader. Rooted in African practice, call-and-response also persisted in African American work songs (such as Jim Cook's chantey above) and continues in congregational response to the preacher in black church practice, in much modern gospel singing, and even in contemporary African American political oratory. Call-and-response, though it runs throughout African American performance, cannot alone explain the survival of the ring shout in Bolden, but it also works synergistically with other forces that have helped to sustain the practice there.

In the shout, the basers overlap the leader's lines in a fashion first described by Allen and give him or her continuous affirmation.[31] As anyone who is considered a good enough singer is allowed to lead, regardless of sex, position, or status (a minister may lead a song if he can but has no more authority than anyone else), the shout is a democratizing force in the community. If the basers do not support the leader sufficiently, there is a breakdown in shared community energy. I have heard Sister Lucille Holloway exclaim, "I don't have the basers!" as she rehearsed a shout song, and her disappointment with the answering singers was more than artistic. In turn, the shouters must be attentive to the words of the song, or they are not properly upholding the singers.

Robert Farris Thompson writes of African leader-chorus singing and dancing:

Rising eloquence can cause the size of the chorus dramatically to swell. But it is not just aesthetic impact that is at issue here, but also the moral condition of the singer or the dancer. Thus a Yoruba refrain:

You are rejected in the town
Yet you continue to sing for them.
If you learn a new song
Who will sing the chorus?

The rights and feelings of others loom very large in African creativity. It does not matter, according to the canon of African call-and-response, how many new steps or verses the person elaborates in his head; if he is of ugly disposition or hatefully lacking in generosity or some other ideal quality. . . . The chorus, as in ancient Attic tragedy, is therefore, a direct expression of public sanction and opinion. . . . Thus call-and-response and solo-and-circle, far from solely constituting matters of structure, are in actuality levels of perfected social interaction. The canon is a danced judgement of qualities of social integration and cohesion. Call-and-response, essentially hierarchic in aesthetic structure, nevertheless perennially realizes, within the sphere of music and of dance, one of the revolutionary ideals of the last century [that of constant self-criticism.] [32]

If one accepts Thompson's linking of African call-and-response to nineteenth-century revolutionary ideals, it is not surprising to see the ring shout flourishing and emerging into national view (through the observers at Port Royal) at the time of the Emancipation. We have seen these forces at work as the Afro-Atlantic shout continually renews and adapts itself within the Bolden community; standards of performance and practice are constantly examined and criticized even as the shout has begun to move from communal celebration and recreation to an entrepreneurial adaptation of an art form with an audience in the larger society. What began as an African practice, forging oneness with the gods and ancestors, adapted itself to Christian worship in slavery in the New World, became a revolutionary force in the nineteenth century, and eventually in the twentieth century became a means of proclaiming the group's identity and history to the outside world through public performance.

The dynamic of call-and-response can be illustrated by Lawrence McKiver's explanation of proper interaction of leader and basers. In 1982 he told us how he planned to lead his group in the singing of "Lay Down, Body" the following day at the Sea Island Festival on St. Simons, two years after he had first organized a group of shouters to perform in public:

If they don't follow you right, on time, not too fast, understand, just time enough for the leader to put their words in—when a song is singing, if the base don't support the shout, the leader, before he put the word in . . . you can't understand the song. Well, you will hear us tomorrow, its . . . an old song . . . we'll be singing "Lay Down, Body," we'll be chopping that one. I imagine, mostly start off on that one, get the crowd off. . . . Anything you gonna do first, to get the attention of people, song will start off like this, I'm gonna sing it and base it:

> Lay down, body,

Understand that? I'm basing, and singing, but I would be saying "tombstone movin'," the baser say, "lay down a little while,"

> Grave is bustin',
> > Lay down a little while
> Soul is risin'
> > Lay down a little while

I would say that two or three times, that's an *express* [expression] in the song, see. The song go beat, beat. There don't be so many words come in, you see, 'cause I come right back to this "body," is the real pointing of the song, you see. I never going too far away from "ol' body," you see. [It] becomes strictly talking personally of a type, like after he die, you know, I mean going to die. . . . I never got anybody to directly describe the song to me, but from the singing of the song, I was so glad to get in and shout it, and sing it with them. . . . They would sing this song, and shout it.

From such explanations as this, and from our observations of public performances of the shout, it seems that there is no weakening of the integrity of meaning of the shout; to the contrary, the public affirmation, the prestige that comes from artistic recognition, and the ability to present a more focused performance by a select and rehearsed group than would be possible in the community all fortify the function of call-and-response song and the power of expressive movement. The aim to "get the crowd off" is not a debasement of the power of the shout tradition, or a decontextualizing of it, but rather a recontextualizing of it with awareness of changing realities. It is a form of the "ethnic intensification" that Barre Toelken has written about, as seen in contemporary Native American powwows. Barre Toelken considers it a "myopic view" to believe that present-day enactments of traditional forms represent "a modern nostalgia for a vanished way of life perpetuated in exercises which lack their 'original' meaning and seriousness. . . . [In] the transmission of cultural reality . . . an idea may be phrased in a number of ways, and indeed it may survive more successfully if it is susceptible of continuous reassessment and retranslation into newer and more functional modes of expression."[33] In the case of the shouters, rather than develop new expressive modes, a restatement of time-honored practices adapted to public performance serves this function.

As mentioned earlier, in 1980 Lawrence McKiver organized a group of singers and shouters from Bolden to perform at the Georgia Sea Island Festival on St. Simons Island; the festival had been presenting early and more modern forms of coastal folklife to the public for several years. Frankie and Doug Quimby, organizers of the festival, were the performing duo that had inherited the title Georgia Sea Island Singers as attrition reduced the once-larger group. With some success the Quimbys had involved the Brunswick African American community in the festival, persuading them that the singing of slave songs and demonstrating such plantation traditions as the beating and fanning of rice were worthy of pride, not better-forgotten practices of passing interest to tourists and summer residents. The Quimbys heard about the ongoing Watch Night shouting in Bolden and met Deacon Jim Cook. Cook in turn contacted Lawrence McKiver, who asked several of the best singers, shouters, and percussion makers in the community to form a performing group. As McKiver tells it,

> *I* am the man that put this group on the road with it. Before every-
> body, everybody round in the community would come on to the
> church . . . but after we going, and I got the little group organize, and
> we went over to the island [St. Simons] and start singing over there
> for Miss [Quimby] and after that, when we got on the road, along with
> her, singing under her wing, she'd say, "You don't have to sing under-
> neath my wing, you got good enough stuff to go take to the public
> yourself, I'll help you and assist you and tell you all the turns." . . . She
> come here and talk with me, and we start spreading and start spread-
> ing till we be as today.[34]

The group, which called themselves the McIntosh County Shouters, were a dramatic success at the Sea Island Festival in 1980 and were invited to the National Folk Festival at Wolf Trap Farm the following year; they performed at the Georgia Folklife Festival in Atlanta and many other events in the years following. The original McIntosh County Shouters, most of whom were grandchildren of London and Amy Jenkins, were: Lawrence McKiver, lead singer; Andrew Palmer, sticker; and Catherine Campbell, Odessa Young, Thelma Ellison, Vertie McIver, Oneitha Ellison, Elizabeth Temple, and Doretha Skipper, basers and shouters. Doretha Skipper occasionally led a song. For the first few years of the group's performing activity, Deacon James Cook accompanied them as a representative of their parents' generation—the first generation born out of slavery—and a spokesperson for the group. He might do a few steps of the shout, and would sing his timber-stowing chantey. At the National Folk Festival, cutting a handsome figure in a three-piece suit, Deacon Cook addressed the "white babies out there, admiring the yesterday tradition," like a nineteenth-century orator, explaining that the shout came to America with his ancestors who were "sold like pigs and cows and sheep"; he said that those days had been left behind, and now we all live "in the only free footstool in God's kingdom." His message was reported in the *Washington Post*.

In their stage performances, until 1994 when Prof. Bettye Ector began functioning as presenter, Lawrence McKiver introduced the songs, often explaining the hidden meanings and references to slavery that had not been revealed previously even to such conscientious observers as Robert Gordon and Lydia Parrish. (At this writing McKiver still introduces some shouts himself.) "Now we can spit it out," McKiver told me in 1980. "I can explain," he said more recently. "If I sing a song, I'm able to tell all of what the song means. That's right. I can do it . . . I like to do that. Really . . . I like to explain to them the meanings of why I sing the song and why my old ancestors—when they sang it, they tell me some of the meanings, and if there is anything more, I can attach them to what the song is about. That's the main thing I like to do."

"You're very good at that," I commented, and guessed that back in the 1930s he wouldn't have been so open to white people.

"They could jump you at any time," he agreed. "[Now] I feel free to anyone who wants to ask me a question about the song I sing. That's an open gap to anyone. . . . I have plenty of college boys and girls, white and black, they'll gang me to ask questions. I like for them to ask. I like to talk with the younger and show them different things, our heritage. That's why I like to go around to the schools."[35]

When asked if there is a different feeling or attitude in stage performances from the traditional shouts in the community, he has always responded that there is no essential difference, but he enjoys and is energized by an appreciative public: "Do I feel different? Naw! I *like* to meet a crowd. I don't say I'm high educated, but I can read and write, and so therefore, for me, the bigger the crowd, the better I like it." Within the community, the shout is not a spontaneous expression of fervor or possession but a conscious art form with clearly articulated standards of performance and a vocabulary of self-criticism. Typical is Odessa Young's statement of why others along the coast, though they might sing shout songs and do some shout steps, do not perform the shout properly: "They can't do it. You might could sing the song, but you can't do it. Because you got to get your foot together. If your feet can't say what the song say, you might as well not to do it. Because it ain't done right. Your feet got to say exactly what that song and stick say, and our feet got to say it exactly—if not, they're not set right. And then everybody can't sing the song right, 'cause they ain't got the voice to sing it. You got to set the song, you can't go sing a song straight out, say you got a shouting song, you ain't got a thing. Not a thing."[36] These standards of performance apply equally to the shout performed in the community on Watch Night and to public performances by the McIntosh County Shouters. Even the younger shouters feel it is necessary to retain the old dialectical pronunciation in the singing of the shout songs.

Carletha Sullivan said, "I give you a good example, [a certain reverend], he tries to sing the shout songs, but he tries to sing it like he speaks, but you can't sing a shout song [like that] you have [to sing it] tossing the words chopped up. . . ."

Freddie Palmer interjected, "You don't try to be too proper, if you do, you mess up." He laughed. "That's all shouting is, natural, an old Negro hymn, walk around 'heb'n,' don't sing 'heaven,' that's the way they used to sing. Used to talk like that. And the shouting songs are the same."[37] This is not antiquarianism but a sense for what is appropriate and what is inappropriate, just as a contemporary Bluegrass musician would not consider it appropriate to use reverb in his amplification.

Pride in being the last to perform the ring shout correctly, and pride in their performance ability, continues to sharpen the skills of the McIntosh County Shouters and validates their decision to do the shout publicly. McKiver recalled performances in Washington, D.C., and at the Black Arts Festival in Atlanta: "Nobody do it like we do it. We with a crew in Washington, they don't have our stuff. South Carolina, something like Johns Island

[Moving Star Hall Singers], they don't have our stuff. We don't find nobody yet—when we hit a stand [festival stage], we draw as much as a big blues stand. We been in Atlanta, and they had some big blues singer from Chicago there, we had more people at our stand, and they was naturally *blowing* the blues! Them black boys was blowing the blues, playing it, too, they didn't touch no effect, didn't pay as much attention as they do us, they follow us from stand to stand. They was interested in what we was doing."[38] Though intensified in the years since the shouters have performed away from the community, pride in gaining recognition from outsiders is not new to the performance traditions the shouters are carrying on. We have seen that observers of the shout and their responses were acknowledged in the days of the Port Royal experiment; and even in African practice, there are frequently spectators, both from the village and outside, at dances and many religious exercises.

The McIntosh County Shouters choose to wear old-fashioned costumes for their stage performances. The women typically wear matching white and green checked long dresses with long sleeves and matching bonnets or African-style print dresses and head rags; the men wear overalls and straw hats or caps. Some observers may consider these costumes overly quaint or contrived, but the shouters do not see it this way. They associate the costumes with the garb of their parents and grandparents and as a way of maintaining a continuity between their ancestors and their art and values. Carletha Sullivan tells an anecdote about her grandmother who taught her much about the old ways:

> She had so many [children], she couldn't drink her coffee in peace. Seriously, she put her coffee underneath . . . back then, all the old ladies used to wear aprons . . . see the dresses we [the McIntosh County Shouters] dress in—they wore dresses down to their ankles. No short sleeves. Because I remember when short sleeves first started to come out, whoo! my grandmother would, "That all yo' ahm out?" They wore long sleeves and dresses down to their ankles, and if they didn't have a bonnet, they had straw hats on, and an apron, and they wore an apron at all times, and she would put her cup underneath her apron and go into the toilet to drink her tea in peace because—I don't know why, we called it the "tea train," the little bit that was left in the cup, we used to beg her for the tea train, and there was so many of us that she

used to go to the bathroom with her tea—in the little outhouse, wasn't no bathroom back then.[39]

Such associations as this create the real context of the shouters' stage performances and costumes. As Henry Glassie has put it, "Context is not in the eye of the beholder, but in the mind of the creator. Some of the context is drawn in from the immediate situation, but more is drawn from memory. It is present, but invisible, inaudible. Contexts are mental associations woven around texts during performance to shape and complete them, to give them meaning."[40]

Above Odessa Young was quoted as feeling that the shout, even today, made her "think where you come from." In this conversation with several of the other shouters in the Mount Calvary annex, I asked her, "Do you think those same thoughts in front of the public, same as you would here?"

"I think about my mother and grandmother and further back, where they come from, so I can get where I am. And my children, how to bring them up, see?" A stage performance of the shout is understood not only as an evocation of the values of the ancestors but as a demonstration of ritualized proper conduct and sense of personal history for the future generations. Several of the other shouters talking with me, along with Odessa Young, agreed that on stage, "You get carried away," and "You don't even see the people sitting out there."

Venus McIver agreed, "Me either!" Then she pointed to Benjamin Reed, "I have to grab the stick and stop him, he gets carried away!"

Amid general laughter, Reed agreed, "You get happy."[41]

Clearly the understood meanings and the salient features and standards of performance carry over from community practice into the stage performances, but some conscious changes have been made by the performing group as the shout was modified in performance for audiences. I asked several shouters, "When y'all do the shout, the different gestures like the 'eagle wing' and [the hand waving in] 'Farewell, Last Day Goin',' did the old people do all those same movements in the old days, or did some of it get added?"

There was some difference of opinion in the responses. Lawrence McKiver said that they (the performing group) "do a lot of the same actions that the older people did." But Odessa Young said, "They shout. That's all they did." She was saying that the older people she had learned from did the dignified shout movement without the more elaborate pantomime and gestures to be seen in the present group's performances.

I persisted in my question. "The old people would just shout? Would they do the 'eagle wing'?"

"Nope," answered Odessa. "They didn't do no 'eagle wing.'"

Margo asked who started the "eagle wing."

"*We* started it," said Odessa. "Our group. When they [the earlier generation of shouters] shout, they shout. They shout happy. But they didn't do an 'eagle wing.'" She did confirm that the old people did indeed perform the actions of "picking up leaves" in the "Eve and Adam" shout. I then inquired about the hip-rocking motion in "Move, Daniel."

Odessa admitted, "The old people used to rock their hip a little bit . . ."

"They didn't rock it out of order," Vertie McIver injected. "They did it orderly. They was so happy about things, and they did it in order. And decent. That's how they did it."

This nice distinction is important in the explanation of a movement that could be seen to resemble the suggestive motions of secular dancing. I then asked why different movements had been added by the performing group.

Bettye Ector answered with one word: "Showmanship."

"We thought it would look better," said Odessa. "The old people didn't do that." Indeed the widely outstretched arms are one of the most striking images of the McIntosh County Shouters' stage performances, yet I had noticed the same gesture at Watch Night shouts in the community. I asked, "You all do . . . the 'eagle wing' on Watch Night, when you're not in a performance. Why is that?"

"It carries on," Carletha Sullivan said.

Bettye Ector added, "It's more or less habit, now."

McKiver put it simply, "We add a little on to the tradition." He did recall that a shouter of his parents' generation, Bo McCullough, did an arm movement to "Move, Daniel." I asked if he did the "eagle wing."

Vertie McIver said, "He might bend his arms . . ."

"The older people, was a different shape," Odessa said. "The old people rock nice and smooth. We can't do it. They was, I don't know, more stronger."

Vertie continued, "Most of them was big. Their flesh was shaking. They do the eagle wing . . . they keep their arms down. We the ones stretch out like that. We the ones stretch out our hands."[42]

Bess Lomax Hawes learned from Bessie Jones and others that the "eagle wing" movement was an integral part of the "Daniel" shout as practiced on St. Simons, and defines it: "Arms bent at elbows are flapped slightly by rotating the shoulder joints in parallel motion. This is the same step as the secular 'buzzard lope' move."[43]

We see now that modifications in the tradition for stage display have moved back into the community. Another addition made since 1994 in the McIntosh County Shouters' stage performances is Bettye Ector's individual introduction of each shouter, who steps forward and briefly executes his or her style of shouting, whether extravagant or restrained. This is another "showmanship" touch, but it reinforces the performance skill and individuality of each performer; it also moves back into community practice.

By the mid-1980s the McIntosh County Shouters had been documented on a Folkways LP and a Georgia Public Television production.[44] This exposure and their successful public performances earned them fame and appreciation. An Atlanta concert promoter called them "the best group in Georgia," placing them in a qualitative arena with successful rock groups, gospel groups, and pop groups. Financial rewards came but were sporadic, and some in the group felt the amounts were disproportionately small given the wide recognition of the group and the uniqueness of the tradition it represented. This is not an uncommon experience of folk professionals, often the finest representatives of their category of culture who find themselves valued less than the best performers in fine art or popular culture. McKiver has remained the leading personality; he has been introduced in recent public appearances as "patriarch of the Shouters" and "a Gullah speaker" by Bettye Ector, and he clearly functions as what is called "artistic director" in other circles. Decisions, however, are made by the whole group: "They can't do without me, and I can't do without them," McKiver said recently. The group has organized itself much as choirs and musical organizations do within African American churches with elected officers; meetings are held to agree upon bookings and fees. While their public performance had maintained artistic and (in Glassie's sense) contextual integrity, it had undeniably become commodified. Remuneration was understandably required for permission to take videos. We had over the years concerned ourselves with the documentation and artistic interpretation of the Bolden shouters, occasionally serving as contacts for performance opportunities and remunerating our friends and informants when grant support made this possible; we never became deeply involved in commercial promotion of the group, leaving this to others. While we maintained friendship and rapport with many in the community, we sensed that some questioned our intentions or wondered why more rewards had not been realized from the group's endeavors.

In 1993 the McIntosh County Shouters were awarded a $10,000 National Heritage Fellowship grant from the Folk Arts Division of the National Endowment for the Arts. They traveled to Washington, D.C., to receive the award, were feted at a ceremony in the Russell Building, and were taken to lunch by their congressman, Jack Kingston. The group receiving this honor was for the most part the same as had been performing since 1980; Carletha Sullivan, daughter of Oneitha Ellison, had joined the group, and Benjamin Reed had replaced Andrew "Bo" Palmer, who had died, as stick man. Nineteen ninety-three marked another less-happy event for the performing shouters. Several members split away from the original group and began to seek performance bookings on their own. Among the complex reasons for the schism are differing opinions about professional management and the desire of the splinter group to recruit performers from beyond the community. This has been a painful period, as the split has affected not just a performing organization, but neighbors and kin who had grown up and seen good and hard times together. When I offered Lawrence McKiver my opinion that it is a pity that the shout, which helped hold the community together in slavery and hard times, was now causing a rift for reasons of managers and money, he tactfully distanced himself: "I'm a peaceable person, I don't like no edgy stuff. . . . So therefore we got good shouters now."[45] As for the new group, the *Atlanta Constitution* reported on a performance in a Jessup, Georgia, recreational center, where old and young African Americans came to see what the reporter later described as "the power and the beauty [the shouters] express to overcome the painful recollections of slavery." Besides the few former members of the original McIntosh County Shouters in the group were several new men and women and a twelve-year-old girl. The "new recruits" told the reporter that learning the shout helped them gain insights into the experience of their slave ancestors; fourteen-year-old spectator Hodari Hopps enjoyed the prowess of the stick beaters and said his first experience with the shout "gets you back to your heritage."[46] Both the original McIntosh County Shouters and the new group perform as frequently in black community centers and churches and in schools as they do in folk festivals and concerts; they may be starting to reseed the shout into the black community beyond Bolden.

Despite the factional rivalries, the New Year was shouted in at Mount Calvary in 1994 with shouters from both groups and members not affiliated with a performance group all in attendance; there were visitors as well. Lawrence McKiver explained that, unlike in earlier years when the shout happened pretty much spontaneously, if dependably, the McIntosh County Shouters group now acts as host and provides refreshments. "When it come to the Watch Night, our group, the McIntosh County Shouters, takes care of the Watch Night. We don't let the church do nothing at all. We save so much and so much of our money through our traveling, to care for our anniversary—we call it our anniversary, but it's for the Watch Night. That's to keep the church from having to put any of their money. . . ." Preachers come and go. In the past, one past pastor tried to suppress the shout and was not retained. According to McKiver, "On Watch Night we don't care anything about taking up money. Some preacher wants to sell you the gospel." He added that "this pastor we have now, he and his wife shout along with us, you ever pay attention, they enjoy it." [47]

Carletha Sullivan reflected on the shout a few weeks afterward: "Yeah, it was . . . like it used to be. Bigger crowd . . . that's the biggest crowd we had for quite a few years now. A few of them were doing it like old times, then most of the younger ones, and some of the older ones, too, didn't really do it like our grandmothers used to do. In fact we [the organized McIntosh County Shouters] don't really do it like they used to. We have the movements, but we are not as smooth as they used to. They were real smooth, and maybe we pick up our feet a little higher than they used to, too, because they used to just kind of shuffle along, move in a shuffling motion. Now Odessa [Young], she kind of do it like the older people, and my mother [Oneitha Ellison]."

Freddie Palmer and Carletha Sullivan have mixed feelings about how much the shout has changed since the McIntosh County Shouters have gone "on the road." I asked whether people in the community feel pretty much the same about the shout tradition now that there is outside recognition.

"I think it changed," Carletha answered.

"It changed," Freddie Palmer agreed.

"I always thought it was something that everyone did. New Year's and Christmas Eve. Until they started going out, and people were just amazed, they had never seen anything like it, and I said, my God, I thought, you know, seriously, I thought it was something everyone did," Carletha explained.

Palmer continued,"I thought it was something everyone did that time of year, Watch Night. And they even made it more popular. But it's not as big as it was back then, but they made it more popular. I am amazed at how far it's going now, those old songs, we used to sing them among ourselves for amusement."

I asked whether the shout has the same function in the community "now that it's gotten more attention?"

Carletha said, "Not really. We do it the same." I inquired about the interest of the kids, and she recalled that when she was a child the shout was a big thing, they got to stay up late. "But now, the kids have so many different things to do till this is of no interest."

Freddie went on to say, "But some of them, they want to know now, when are we gonna pass it on to them. I say, 'Y'all got to come out. Come on out, and you can learn the song.' My daughter, she asked me that question the other day, when are we gonna pass it on to them. I said, 'You got to get with Lawrence. . . .'" The activity of the performing group has also stimulated interest among the "younger kids." "They have been inspired by them, by places they've been, places they've been invited to go. That inspired a lot of our young people. They didn't figure it would go that far. But now since they brought that big award back to the church. That was lovely." Then the conversation turned to people in the middle generation, to whether they might join the Shouters.

Carletha referred to her cousin sitting beside her. "Now he's good, Freddie. I don't know about beating the stick, but he can clap, he can clap enough by himself for everybody. Seriously, he can make enough noise by himself, that we wouldn't need another clapper if he was there. He can sing, and he can clap, I don't know what he can do with the stick. And he can shout." They talked some more about how everybody can't set a shout song. Freddie Palmer said, "Benjamin [Reed] get that stick right on!"

Carletha added, "Mostly if Lawrence get it set, Harold Lee or Jerry can take it over. . . ."

Freddie modestly claimed not to be a "good songster," but Carletha contradicted him. "But I like to do it," he said. "But it's in the blood. Can't get away from it."[48]

The shouters remain guardedly optimistic about whether the younger generation will take up the shout. The stick seems to hold an attraction. Carletha told me, "The shout, because we do it every Watch Night, they come out, they catch on, some of the little boys, they grab the broom or whatever, and beat it."

Venus McIver laughed, "The first time my son heard it, he beat that broom two solid weeks in that room, I tell you! Two solid weeks, every day!"

"Think he'll come back on Watch Night, keep it going?" I asked.

"They'll remember, and the ones that's interested, they'll pick it up . . . it won't be hard, they pick it up and go right on. And some of the kids, they get the movements and stuff good."[49]

The shout in Bolden is probably just what its performers consider it to be, the last holdout of the classic ring shout along the southeastern coast. More than that it is unique in being a viable religious tradition in an African American community that continually and specifically references continuity with Africa, slavery, and Emancipation as elements interlocked with worship and oneness with the Spirit. Through persuasive and eloquent public performances, the shouters of Bolden now share this tradition with the rest of us; this is their gift to us, at once humbling and enlightening.

Shout, 1987–1997. Charcoal, 22 in. × 30 in. Collection of the artist.

"Farewell, Last Day Goin'," 1992. Charcoal, 38 in. × 50 in. Collection of the artist.

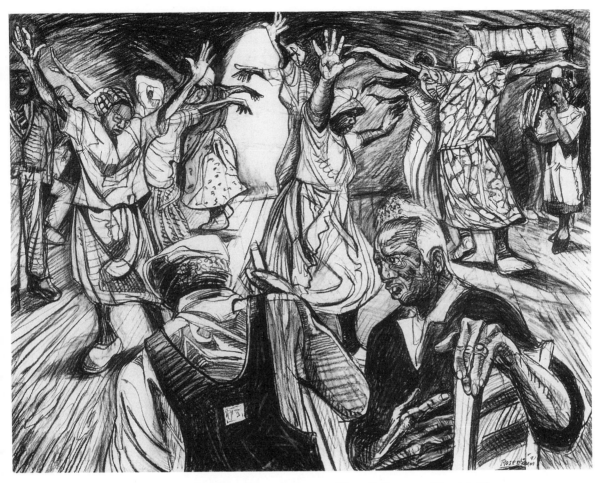

"Do the Eagle Wing, Daniel," 1991. Charcoal, 38 in. × 50 in. Collection of Patricia Thorne, Atlantis, Florida.

"Time Drawin' Nigh"—Reverend Palmer at the Shout, 1992. Charcoal, 38 in. × 50 in.
Collection of Andrew Ladis, Athens, Georgia.

"Pickin' Up Leaves," 1992. Charcoal, 38 in. × 50 in. Private collection, Athens, Georgia.

Shout at the Morton, 1994. Charcoal, 38 in. × 50 in. Collection of Jim and Sharon Campbell, Greenville, South Carolina.

"Farewell, Last Day Goin',*"* 1992. Charcoal, 38 in. × 50 in. Collection of Rick Johnson,
Athens, Georgia.

Children's Shout, 1992. Charcoal, 38 in. × 50 in. Collection of the artist.

Clappers and Sticker on Watch Night, 1994. Charcoal, 38 in. × 50 in. Permanent collection, Fine Arts Center, Greenville County School District, Greenville, South Carolina.

McIntosh County Shouters, 1983. Oil on canvas, 64½ in. × 70 in. Georgia Museum of Art, University of Georgia; transfer from the Georgia Sea Grant College Program, School of Marine Programs. GMOA 96.84.

3 Lawrence McKiver, Boss Songster

My mother lived to be 104 years old, and she have five more sisters besides her. And they all like to keep the old slave shout going around in the community. We alway shout the . . . New Year in, shout the old year out. And she—they was sitting around and sometimes they be making quilts through the fall of the year after they done take in all their crops. . . . People have something to keep themselves warm in them old houses, and they'll start telling stories of what their mother tell them. Well I being a small-size boy, I be taking in all that stuff, you know. And that's the way I come to be carry it on today.

—Lawrence McKiver

As Lawrence McKiver approaches his eightieth year, he lives alone in a small house set back off the highway in Bolden—under the live oak trees. With some of his extra earnings from taking the shout out of the community in recent years, he screened in his front porch, eliminating the green and white sawtooth ornamental woodwork that had distinguished the house from several other modest neighboring houses, and added a carport. The interior is dark and sparsely furnished. In the back is a small kitchen; there is an iron heater and a brass bedstead in the middle room; on the walls of the front room are posters of folk festivals he has appeared at with the McIntosh County Shouters, photos of the group, and one old photograph of his mother, Charlotte Evans. Lawrence is more likely to be out in the dirt yard than in the house, talking to a group of young neighbors. One time we stopped to see him in the winter as men were returning from hunting. "I'm kin to everything you see here," he said, indicating both the younger and older men milling around.

"I'm the boss" of the shouters, he says, and none would deny it. Not that he makes the final decisions—these are made by the group and community—but he is the man who indeed "knows all the songs," is in full possession of the shout song repertoire, and is the person most knowledgable about the shout in all its aspects—with the possible exception of Reverend Palmer, who is inactive in the shout. Knowledge brings power in traditional societies, and McKiver is in secure possession of both. He speaks of his mother and his "aunties" as his "old ancestors" and draws wisdom and authority from them. As he speaks his expressively chiseled features and his choppy, often repetitive but forceful phrases convey urgency, and his hands dance in delicate gestures that amplify the meanings of his words: the visitor as well as the kinsman *must* understand. He is the "big" singer in Bolden, and the man with the fullest knowledge not only of the shout but of the rich fabric of folklife of which the shout is a part. And he is not just a bearer and repository of tradition, he renews it in practice, shapes and refines new performing modes. He has reworked some of the shout songs and has made new solo songs that express his religious faith and comment on the social turmoil and drug culture that have moved into his community. We have heard already about and from him, with regard to the shout, in these pages. Now let us flesh out his story further, through mostly his own words.

Oh, I was born in 1915. April the eighteenth. Really, in fact, I was born on Easter Sunday morning, but you can't plug a Easter Sunday morning, understand, so then I placed my birthday on April eighteenth, so I'd be celebrating in between each one. . . . My mother had six head of us, and I don't know anything about a daddy; I never seen my daddy in my life. My mommy told me my daddy died two weeks before I was born. All I know is my mommy, and I know what she had to go through to take care of us. She would work for a white fella down there, call him Kelly Townsend, sometimes get twenty-five cents, some sweet potato, some syrup.[1] [Charlotte Evans worked in the fields for Townsend.] And from that, she would get those white folks' clothes down there, and put 'em on her head, and tote 'em here, and wash 'em and starch 'em and iron 'em and tote 'em back down there, and maybe she might get two dollars and a half, and a quarter, I'm not lying. They didn't have money to pay her, that much. . . . That was big money in that time. Because you could go and buy a piece of meat for fifteen cents, a piece of bacon, you could buy a big package of grits, flour, sugar, tea, you could buy different stuff like that.[2]

Lawrence described the house he grew up in and working in the fields as a child:

Me and Reverend Palmer was talking about that last Sunday. Them old houses, we had paper pasted on the side of the wall, any old paper we could get, you take some flour dough, and we cook it into a starch, and we stick paper on the walls. Old board windows. Shingles on the top, cypress shingles. We didn't have no tin on the top, and such stuff as they got on these houses now. Natural cypress shingles, they be about this wide, and while they dry, you could lay down in your bed, yes, you could see the stars, that's true, and see the stars. And when it come a rain, it might leak a little while, but when the shingles swell they come back together, not a drop of water come in no more. You could peek through the crack, see the sky, see the clouds moving across the sky, the stars up there, but when that shingle get wet, it come together, that's it! No more water coming in. We lay down on a straw mattress on the floor, we didn't have no bed. . . . Yeah, I come up on the rough side of the mountain. Sometimes I go to church, they be singin' a song, "Comin' Up on the Rough Side of the Mountain." I said, "Y'all don't think y'all know something about the rough side of the mountain!"[3]

    . . . all through that we worked the fields. We made our own syrup. We raised hogs. We killed the hogs, smoke 'em, we learn how to do that, and if we didn't have enough meat to last us through the year we walk to go, and we plant onions and stuff, and my mama would cook a pot of grits or what they have. And we would walk cross here with a sack, in winter time go down to the creek, catch crabs, we bring the crabs back, we might get a good bundle of crabs. We bring that back to the house, she back them crabs, take off all them back, take off all the "dead man," break off the foots, and then she take them . . . and put 'em in the pot, and she cut up onions over them crabs, or garlic or something like that—she could cook—and make a gravy, put it over our grits, and then we go to the field, go to work. We got to go to school, we walk to where the Buccaneer is now [a restaurant]. We walk just about to the Buccaneer, that's a good two miles and three quarter, to a house. . . . The old lady, we called her Miss Ella Hills, we go to her house. She had a little learning and she would teach us, and we hit the road, and we walk back. That's the way we get our learning. We didn't know nothing about those other kind of school. Not when I was a boy. They had one little book. Boys then, they didn't wear no long pants . . . your pants is cut off here, and put a strap on them, you blouse 'em here. When you wearing long pants, you seventeen, eighteen years old. . . . Just fighting my way, me and my brother, and a bunch more around us, we go to the school, come back home take off our pants. We had, we called 'em old cow-belly Brogans, we didn't wear them, you put them aside, and we go in the field, we work the field.

You erect the fence. Cattle used to be out in the woods, they would jump in the field and eat up the stuff. You would erect around the fence inside and outside, then you go and build the fence round and round where the cows won't jump in. Then get the dead one, put it in the fields for fertilizer, and we get the live one, green pine straw, put it in the horse stable so the horse pound that as he walk round there. And we would go and put that straw out there, and we would plow that in. It rotten. We didn't use Purina, anything like that, we used horse stable fertilizer. And we get the chicken coop fertilizer, and we streak that down the road, and then we bed that in, specially for pota-toes and cane. [Cane] can grow here . . . they grow so high till they bend over and come back down. And put 'em underneath the corn and potatoes. We make some of the stuff to help us survive. We have so much chicken. But you don't get a chicken every day and Sunday too. Sometimes I get a beating, but I broke a chicken leg so she can cook it, but I be sorry after I did it, I didn't get none of the choicy parts. Some of the neck, the foot, something like that, backbone. I still thought I had something. I get a good whitewash, they call it. She'll whip you darn good, my mommy. . . . I get to run the chicken . . . I goes to break a chicken leg, that's bad luck for me, my backside! Sometimes the leg ain't broke too good, she take that chicken, get those three little sticks, and some string, and she put it around that chicken's leg, that's one of her good chickens, she splice that hen's leg, let her hen live. But I be wanting 'em to kill 'em. See. She splice that hen leg. She don't splice my back, she whip my back!

After school and work the children in the community would enjoy ring plays and other singing games. They have faded away in Bolden, but they are fresh in the memory of Lawrence McKiver and others of his generation. They had a good time at one of our recording sessions in 1981 recreating the movements of "Billy Arbor" and "Lost Mama's Needle." McKiver remembers doing the ring plays of his childhood:

Yeah, that was our life back in them times be five or six of us, maybe sometimes seven or eight of us, girls and boys. We had an aunt we called Aunt Sarah. She was a small lady . . . but she was supple as a wet dishrag. She could dance and she good songster too. My mother's baby sister. And she do all them old songs. . . . See how this song go: the girls get on one side of the line and the boys be on the next side of the line. Get down there and say, had a song say

> Lost mama' needle, doodle, doodle do
> Help me to find it, doodle, doodle do
> Oh, swing your lover, doodle, doodle do
> Oh, swing your lover, doodle do.
> Go yonder, uh-huh, go yonder, uh-huh
> Carry 'em home, uh-huh
> Carry 'em home, uh-huh
> Carry 'em home, uh-huh

And keep on down the line. This boy and this girl, they get down between the two line and they be in each other arms and swing 'em round this way and swing 'em round this way here. See, first start off say lost mama needle, say help me to find it. Say scratch with your right foot. Then say scratch with your left foot. And then after while they say swing your lover. Keep on down the line swinging 'til they go on down the other end of the line. Then the next two, he grab his girl and they do the same thing, keep going down, keep going down, 'til the whole line going through. And it be really beautiful.[4] Then we had one we call, "We Will Set This Little Red Bird in the Chair." We get one of the prettiest girls we got, see. We set her in the middle . . . and go round, start circlin' round in a ring. Say

> We will set this little red bird in the chair, in the chair
> She have lost all the fruit that she have last year,
> Rise, Sally rise, wipe your weeping eyes,
> Fly to the east, Sally, fly to the west,
> Fly to the very one that you love the best.[5]

Then she fly to the boy, see. When say fly to the one you love the best, regardless of who is in front of her, that's the one she would fly to. That might not be the boy she loved. Maybe it be the girl she love, but she go to that one, you see. So the boy, while you singing that song, the boy who like her, he try to be in front of her at the time. That be the girl he wants to see . . . I try to go around that ring fast enough to be in front of her, that was the trick about the song, you see.

These ring plays of the southern blacks, like the play parties of rural southern and midwestern whites, blurred the distinction between childhood singing games and games of adolescent and young adult courtship. Their euphemistic names—"ring plays" and "play parties"—and the fact that they moved to the participants' singing and not to such worldly instruments as fiddles, banjos, and later guitars, kept them just shy of being considered dances and thus being subject to condemnation by the church. The shout, as we have seen, is descended from African religious dances and is related to African American secular dances and plantation walk arounds, as well as to ring plays. But as Lawrence McKiver was initiated into the ways of the shout as a boy, he quickly learned the difference between dancing and shouting. He watched the old sisters moving in the ring to the strains of "Move, Daniel": "They say they doin' the 'eagle wing,' they . . . be going around in a circle . . . like a bird flying, see. Like a bird flying. . . . Then they come back and say go the other way. They stop and they be going around righthand way, they come back and go lefthand way. Then after while say 'rock, Daniel, rock,' all of 'em go to shaking their hip. Keep going right on around in a circle, see. . . . But every time the song make a different statement they gotta stop and go the direction the song say." I suggested that some people might say this looks like a dance, which prompted the familiar nice distinction:

> It's not a dance. It's not a dance. You wouldn't dare to cross your legs. I was a boy round nine or ten years old, and I be wanta do the shout.[6] I always did like to sing, I always did like "Move, Daniel," I did, I wanted to see the people doing it, them old folks with them long dresses on. I didn't know the motion of the song. Daniel have a lot of moving in it, the leader call, the shouters got to react to the call, and then they say "go the other way," and I be little crazy, I didn't know how to go back with the people, and them old folks, they didn't take much time, just catch you back, gonna shove you out the ring. And they going on back the other way, like the song

> > Move, Daniel, move, Daniel
> > Go the other way, Daniel,
> > Rock, Daniel, rock, Daniel

> When it say rock, them old folks they be rocking and going on like this, and they change to all the different commands of the song. 'Cause they was serious in what they be doing, they could do it, they had an old man they call, we call him Bo McCullough, he had a heavy voice, he could sing [imitates]:

> > Do the eagle wing, Daniel
> > Move, Daniel, move, Daniel

> He come in with a voice like that, some of the lighter voice have it a while, and then he come in, then another one catch it, and keep all round like that, fine voice. Come around to that bass voice again, and I tell you the straight truth, they have that church ringing.[7]

Of all the shouters he remembers from his boyhood, Fannie Ann Evans was "best in the business." He repeated:

> The best in the business. It would do you good to see her shout. . . . She had enough flesh on her bones you know to keep the rhythm, you know. You take a person with good flesh on her bones, she was a well-built woman. She had a nice hip, you know, and she was super. She could just get around. She could shout so good. It would do you good

to see them old folks, have them long dress on, come along. They could really put it on.[8]

Sister Evans was shouting and rocking to "Goin' Down Heaven, Easy Walk," and a youthful Lawrence McKiver was appreciating a sublimated sensuality in the shout, flowing into his time from the African roots of the shout where generative motions of the human body and movement in holiest worship were not seen as contradictory. The special conventions of the shout made the "holy dance" acceptable in the church, in the context of Christian belief.

Perhaps the persistence and acceptance of the shout, along with the courting "plays" during Lawrence McKiver's adolescence in Bolden, allowed his community to be more permissive than some about frolics and dancing. He recalls these as being enjoyed, in their proper time and place, even by church members and shouters. Like many accounts of African American frolics of that era, McKiver's reflects sporadic instances when the rougher crowd injected fear and violence into what was usually friendly community entertainment.

> Back in my teen age, you know, boyhood days, we didn't think about girls too much, we play around girls. If we courted, have to be very sly; say the old folks, they didn't allow that kind of jive. You mannish rascal, you! See, then after I come up to be teen-ageified, a little more modernified, yeah, I'll tell you, that I wasn't a sport. I feel like I was. That after I come up around the eighteens and the twenties, I been working ever since I was thirteen, I would give my mama money, I would buy my clothes . . . she give me so much and so . . . and I would stay sporty! Yeah, I tell no lies at that, I stay real sporty. I was a good dancer, sing the blues, and a good liar—to the girls. You can't be a sport unless you a good liar. You can't have no womens unless you a good liar. I got to be smart, I try to like all the girls, there's a big dance somewhere, I figure they all gon' be there, I ain't goin'. I want to go, the other boys, when my favorite girl was there, I say go on with them, man. I have one in that crew I like better than the others. I didn't want to get there and get to meet all them girls together, they would catch me in a lie, see, I wouldn't go. I don't go. I was a good liar and a sport. I sport a lot, was a good dancer, could sing the blues. But I never did learn to play music, I wouldn't be here talking with you today, 'cause I'd a made something for my own self. [In those days] yeah, when I

was fourteen, they would have house frolics, they call it. They would have peppermint candy, they would break 'em up in pieces, give it to you for a nickel, but a nickel was hard to get, and you could get a glass of parched peanuts for a nickel or a dime.[9]

This peppermint candy was called "Long John." There were no "guitars . . . and all that fine stuff they got now" at the frolics. Lawrence's sister, Gussie, who was also a fine church singer and baser in the shout, made music for the frolics on a pan.

She would beat the bake-pan. She could beat one! Make all the music you want with that bake-pan. Get in a corner somewhere, and get on that bake-pan, and she'd make all kind of music, you could believe that she could do it. That's the way we would have house dance. Oh, she was good at it. She could sing. That's the way we have our frolic enter-tainment . . . and she could astonish you.[10] [Lawrence's sister sang "old bluesy songs," and he would] cut the buck. . . . See, I was in my teens . . . see, I was fast as a squirrel, then, I don't care what you say. I didn't feel like a guy could beat me dancing. . . . I used to cut the buck . . . when I was more young, and more supple, I could cut just as much buck as any Mister Man, make like the mule bucking, like the mule trying to throw you off, and every such stuff as that, and be mocking the mule, hold the mule

Whoa, mule, stop cuttin' you fool

And my foot'd be playing a tune, and my foot'd be patting, just like that, and some of them have a stick, and see which one could beat the other. . . .[11]

I cut the buck a while, another little boy see if he could beat me and be going on around just like that. Then we come back and we do the Charleston. One we think the best get the biggest piece of candy.

Well after on up through the later days the bigger boys, they go to them old log camps and different places like that, cutting ties, they go on them different gangs and working different things, they come back in and . . . have a frolic. I can remember some them old boys, one they called Pompey McCullough and a tall man they called Long John and all them. They come in, they roll a pin 'round their foot kind of tight

like that and they have them a cap with a long bill on. They could turn
the party out, see. Have old kerosene lamp in there. Tell there gonna
be a row, be a fight. . . . Old Pompey come in there. He tall, had
pretty hair, pretty curly hair, big arms. And he come out there, say,
"Tell them we gotta start getting to the door 'cause ain't gonna be
long gonna be some running done." And he come in there and he said
[hollers]

> Hey, lawd, hey lawd, hey
> Hey, lawd, hey lawd, hey

And he get on the floor and start cutting the buck and the whole house
be shaking, you know, just shaking. It won't be long then the other one
come in, Long John come in, start a fight then, after while he pull in
the whole party. Knock the lamp off, take all your peanuts, anything
they could get hold of. Get up and start a fight, you see. Everybody
scared of 'em. You gotta run and get out the way to close up the party.
Boy he tough. Yeah.[12]

[Again recalling the frolics of his youth]
That was the fun back in my young days . . . I would float out, be a
man, and I'd float out. I would sing the blues, and sometimes when
I would be round them joints dancing with the women, I was a
pretty good dancer. Had me an old piece of car then, dressed good,
didn't have much money, but didn't take much money to do then,
'cause if there's a dance in a jook joint, well you could get in for a
dollar.

Dances and frolics, as well as church through the year and shouts at Christmas and New Year's, were respite from a life of grueling labor. From the
farmwork of his childhood and early adolescence, McKiver went to work as
a commercial fisherman.

I start fishing, I reckon, I was up around my last teens. . . . It was
tough have to pull the net in by hand. And your hand be sore and you
have to buck the boats. (Sometimes your hand be so sore till you can't
hardly unbutton your pants to pee.)[13] Sometime the old engine'll shut
off on you, and you gotta go down there and crank it. And that was a

miserable ship then when that engine set off. You out there and the boats overboard and you gotta pull the boats by hand. [You] have to go down there fight that old Buick engine, that old Chrysler engine. Fume from that gas make you seasick. Then you wish you died. Miserable, I tell you.

But now after they come up, the mens get more wiser, then they put a vent in the boat. One time they take the old rope, wrap it around a spool on the outside and you can pull your doors up. Then they come from that 'til they get the big boats where you got your winch. Got your winch, you pull up, where the doors come up, stop it right there and drop it, go back and get your whip line and come back and put it on the spool, pull your bag on up to you. Then you take the lazy line . . . then you come back and take your whip line and take your bag down where the shrimps at. . . . They have different sign, different time of the tide, the moon, you know. When the springtime come up first time, high tide, that's the sign the fishermen use. . . . After cold snap in the wintertime, they'll go out and make good catches then. . . . But the shrimps, shrimps a thing that scientists now try to figure them out, but they can't figure out all about a shrimp. You can go out today and don't find none and go tomorrow and find a bunch. Shrimping is a thing I did for a long while. Had catches in big quantity. Hauled 'til my hands be so sore 'til blood come out.[14]

McKiver fished on a boat called the *Captain Kidd,* and so many others he can't remember all the names. He worked for good captains and bad—those he called good gentlemen and others who would cheat the men. He went around Key West and in the Gulf as far as Campeche, Mexico. In port prostitutes and pickpockets would sometimes get "a thousand, fifteen hundred dollars" from some of the men.

But never none did get me 'cause I never was a whiskey drinker. I don't drink it. I get my money, they can't get none but little bit I want them to have. I have seen them fellas come in there from Campeche on a good trip . . . be fishing at night, sleeping the day, and they come in drink that whiskey, get tight, and go to bed with some of them women. They wake up the next morning, the women be gone and all they money be gone. They don't see her no more. But never have happen to me. I been in Fort Myers, seen a man walking the street want buy a pack of cigarettes, couldn't buy breakfast. . . . They have to go back to the boat and eat.

Lawrence may have fished by the signs of the moon, but he does not consider himself superstitious. His "mama never kept too much for signs . . . she never did care too much for signs. She just go along and pray." Likewise, while his mother did not believe in root doctors, she did "dig herbs like snakeroot and a weed they call boneset and feverweed. And get the leaves off the elder bush or the palm of Christian leaf, and wrap us if we have a fever and give us that old bitter weed. And it kill the fever."[15] He believes there is a place for traditional remedies and for modern medicine but turns to prayer in time of deepest need, as the time his wife became ill.

I believe the best remedy for any individual in this life is you get off in a private place and ask for what you want . . . in my trouble, I go to God . . . get in my room away from everybody and I get on my knees and pray to God. And I know my wife was sick, I couldn't find out what was the matter with her. I take her to every doctor I knowed. I spent every penny I had, little saving I had. I couldn't never find. Doctor eat me up in every way. I just walk across over there and get on my knee and ask God before my wife leave off this world to let her sickness be made known. Because my people had believe that somebody had fix her or something like that. And it wasn't a thing but she had sugar. And I went to Dr. Jordan over there, colored doctor in Savannah right now. He's a real doctor. He find out that she had sugar. And there wasn't a beautifuller black lady than she. That's her picture right there now.

Lawrence's wife died in 1962; his wife was Anna Mae Palmer, the sister of Doretha Skipper. The couple married in 1934. Lawrence is father of two children: a son who lives in Florida and a daughter who works in the post office in Hinesville, Georgia.

In a way similar to the accommodation he had worked out in his mind between church and the shout and such worldly amusements as dancing, Lawrence is devoutly Christian and yet remembers encounters with spirits and haints (ghosts) from his childhood.

They would tell us stories about haints. This whole hill really was an Indian territory, believe it if you want to. . . . Old board house, you know, board windows. Me and my brother, we sleep on the floor. And right along the wall, an old road be along there, the old railroad tram came through there. Near back in 1911. But before that was an old wagon road come right along there. And I could witness different things with ghosts myself. . . . You could hear, something like a trace chain, you know, them old trace chain hitch the horse up with. You be hear it coming down that old road just as plain as one, two, three. I guarantee you, this is no joke about this now. You could hear it at certain time of the month—you could hear the horse, boom, boom, boom, coming right along here. Old trace chains rattling on top the wagon. One night me and my brother was hot, we had the window open, old board window open. And I was laying down on our old staw mattress. We laying down on the floor. My first cousin was over on one side of me and my brother was on the other side and I be in the middle in right center of the window. And I hear something go like a horse eating grass, you know. I set there awhile and I listened and I listened at it and after awhile, I did look up to the window. There was something indicate a mule was stand up right over here. You oughta see me getting out from there. That's a real fact. That's no joke about that. This place used to be really ghostified. You could walk down through there and see something coming along, plodding along just like a person. Look like it be up off the ground. Just glide along. It was no imitation. You would a had to walk along there and you see that man coming along through there, that old settlement right up here. You see him, I guarantee you. But since the settlement get more thicker, the people get more thicker, things like that vanish away from 'round here. I witnessed that for myself.

I believe it was old Indians' ghosts, you know, that's what I believe it was. . . . You could up there dig up old Indians, old Indian parts, be little old thin, made out of clay, something like clay, but it be hard. You could dig up whole pieces, that's no lie.[16]

Lawrence McKiver served in the army during World War II, but his service for his country did not keep him from feeling the indignities of Jim Crow. He recalls an incident in 1941:

I went to the drug store in Brunswick, Georgia, and bought a Co-Cola, and I bought the soda, and I was drinking it as I come out the store. And this little dude, he didn't want me to take a drink of the soda inside the store, and I buy it in the store. He run out there with a broom, he want knock me with it. I tell him, "You looking at the wrong man. If you reach at me with that broomstick, you might miss it and hit at me." I'd caught him and mopped the place with him. I weighed about 185 pound, and I'm good with these, right on.[17]

He showed the smooth skin over his knuckles. He added, "I don't like violence." He was glad for the "King Movement" of the 1960s:

[Martin Luther King] wasn't for violence. He wanted every one to be treated alike. You come in my house, I'm gonna treat you like my niece inside there, or Carletha, or any of the boys out there, or the Shouters. But some of the people didn't understand King. The King Movement didn't want to put the white over the black or the black over the white. He wanted everyone to be treated as a human. But a lot of the whites, special' in the south parts, Alabama, Mississippi, Louisiana, back in them places they would want me to go to a business place, they give me my food out there [in the back]. You can go in and eat, I can't go in and eat. I'm a human like you.[18]

After his service in the army, McKiver went back to commercial fishing. Eventually he quit fishing so that he could take care of his mother in her last years; he dreaded the idea of his mother outliving him and not having him to care for her. This did not come to pass; she died on Watch Night 1979 at the age of 104. Lawrence's bedrock Christian faith, and most of his knowledge of the shout, spiritual songs, and his people's history, he learned from her. His favorite song is a spiritual his mother sang:

Oh when the train come along,
Oh when the train come along,
I want to be, be at the station,
Oh when the train come along.

Church, I'm not talkin' about this old earthly train,
I mean the trains that the saints all ride,

I want to meet it at the station
Oh when the train come along.[19]

Lawrence joined the church as a boy and has been a faithful member ever since, though he remains somewhat apart from the official church hierarchy: he never became a deacon. His faith is expressed in prayer, in testimony, through the shout, and through his greatest talent, song. He has been a member of the choir and is called upon frequently to offer a solo song during services. These songs are usually of his own composition and do not focus on Scripture as much as they do on faith, morality, and in perfecting a personal relationship with God. One is called "I Want to Live a Life That Will Be Pleasing in Your Sight." Another goes:

Oh, when trouble rise in your home
There ain't no need for you to weep or moan.
Although sometimes I know you feel like you's all alone
But just remember that God is still on His throne.
Oh, yes, God is still on His throne.
        You get down on your knees,
Tell Jesus all about your troubles.
Jesus can fix it for you,
Oh, yes, He can, I know He will
'Cause He said He will fight your battle
If you just stand still.

Why don't you just tell Jesus all about your troubles
And let Jesus fix it for you
'Cause there ain't no one down here will fix it like He will do;
He got a master key, and He know right where all your troubles be.
He knows your troubles from A to Z
You don't have to beg Him, He will fix it for free . . .

Others of Lawrence's compositions address moral problems that concern him greatly as social disorganization becomes more pronounced. Illegal drugs are besetting rural communities like Bolden as well as urban areas, and Lawrence composed a song that he calls his "dope song."

That dope song! I'll sing that. I made pretty good many dollars for that song. Folks went by, tip me ten, tip me high as twenty dollars for that song. Write it not too long ago. I would look at the dope guys, out there in that park. I could look at you and size you up, write a song, watching after you a few days, see how you react. . . . You can't think hard of me, I'm just telling the truth about the song:

You know, it's a shame, a shame, a shame, a shame,
God knows, it's a shame, how drugs destroyed so many
    young folks down here in this lan'

You know the government's doin' everything that it can,
It give food stamps and money, just for a helpin' han'
But they won't stand on the po' little hungry children,
They're tradin' it all out to the drug sellin' man,
    You know it's a shame, etc.

You know they picked up a habit that they can't support,
And they will do anything just for a little piece of dope,
    You know, etc.

You know they walk all day, and they walk all night
Searchin' for door to door,
Tryin' to borrow a dollar just to buy some more,
    You know, etc.

You know they don't have time to even change their clothes,
They standin' on the block, beggin' for a dollar just to buy a piece of rock,
    You know, etc.

You know they don't want to work no more,
There ain't no job that can please their mind.
They just lay around to rob, kill, beg, and steal,
    You know, etc.

You know they don't have no age at all, but they sho' don't look young
    no mo'
They done sniffed so much coke until they sho' is a walkin' ghost,
    You know, etc.

You know drugs related, she done made her score,
She got the jail so full they can't hold no more
    You know, etc.

When he makes such songs as this, Lawrence seldom writes them down. Using a cassette tape recorder, he says he "put the song down, I get my words to blend in, match in. . . . I never forgot a song once I sing it. My memory is just that good so far."[20]

Lawrence McKiver has a critical temperament and a sense of artistic and moral rightness that informs all his judgments. In his later years he has striven to build on his limited formal education by attending night school; he is proud that he can work math problems correctly and can put his "words to place, if I just take my time. I know past tense, just as well as present." He is alluding to the speech of the old people who "didn't have book learning." Like Carletha Sullivan, he never heard the term Gullah until it was used by outsiders in recent years, and he sometimes rejects the pejorative term "Geechee" that frequently is applied to the coastal dialect.

> Nobody around in this community would call it Geechee. That's just their everyday thing, understand? Say . . . after you pass South Carolina, up around Virginia, Washington, the northern states, they say we Geechee, because we talk more flatter, we don't take time to dip a word, aaarrah this aarrah that.[21] We just say this or that, and we go on about our business. My mama say "come 'er' gal, come eh boy," somewith like that. "What ye do sucha thing fo', I tell you not tuh do dat." See, understand when I first went into New York, I went on the stage, and I was talking, I explained something for them. I said, "Now listen, I know what you callin' me, a G.G., that means to say I'm a Georgia Geechee, understand." I say, "I may sound funny to you, you sound funny to me."[22]

The shout has moved in its shuffling yet proud circular path through Lawrence McKiver's life. It has been both a renewal and a paradox for him: there is scarcely a word in the shout songs or a step in the shout that does not carry a "remembrance" from slavery and those who have struggled and died in the hard old days:

> In this field we must die,
> As sho' as you live, you born to die.

Yet, he does not think his mother and aunts and uncles were thinking about slavery times when they sang those words.

They were just doing something to keep their mind off the past tense, you know. It was mostly a rejoicing thing, for them. It was their happiness. They didn't sing it for nothing at all sad. The words of the song related to so many true things, understand, but they didn't take it as they were studying about their parents born in slaves—my mama didn't born in no slave, but her mama, they was born in that. The shout is a thing just come falling down through the generation of our people, understand. So . . . they take it as a rejoice.

. . . You come on down through the generation with the shout, I don't think any one in our group looking back with animosity of what has happened to our people back then. I know I'm the one that got the songs alive today. So far as I can see. I don't sing the song as a memory, as a grudge. I'm just remembering what my mommy told me how they had to come up. But I'm not doing it as a remember, as a grudge about how they was treated. 'Cause I can't tote that, I can't tote that. I got to tote a clear mind, so I can meet my God for myself.

Regardless of who you is, where you from, who you are, if you's a person, you's a person—if you're not a good person, you're not a good person. If you're a person full of foolishness, I don't have time for foolishness. I might laugh and tell you an old story, joke, like sometimes I walk out among the boys, I tell an old story, joke. We laugh at the joke, but if I find one out there drinking whiskey, talking nonsense, I come in my house. Like a person drinking whiskey, he can't talk sensible things. . . . I say, "You ain't talking, your whiskey talking." But if you come to me, you talking with sense, I sit down here hours and hours and talk with you. Like when you and your wife come here, I talk hours with you all, 'cause you didn't come to talk nonsense, and I don't mind talking with a person on my heritage. I can bravely talk about my heritage, because my people come over the rough side of the mountain. Understand?

Lawrence McKiver is optimistic that the shout will be carried on by young people. He reflected on the Watch Night shout of 1994:

To me the shout was just as good as I would like to see. We had more young people. . . . They taking it up real good. When you see Watch Night, if you notice, we have more young people doing the shout, the old people can't hardly get on the floor. I think they like it. In our group, we're gonna have a young person. . . . We's gonna be the McIntosh County Shouters until I die. Then y'all [the others] can take it, do what you want . . .[23]

Lawrence McKiver is not really nonchalant about the future of the practice that has animated his spirit, voice, and bones from youth to old age. Though he brilliantly "rephrased," in Barre Toelken's sense, the ring shout into a public performance vehicle for communicating his community's history and values to the larger public, he understands that if the practice is to have continued viability, it will inevitably be reworked and adapted to new times by others. Rev. Nathan Palmer, the only living member of his community with comparable depth and breadth of knowledge of the shout, declined to do what McKiver did—to expand the practice of the shout beyond the community in public performance. Through the efforts of McKiver and his "crew," the shout turned the corner and will have some kind of ongoing life, though it will inevitably become more distanced from the textures of the lives of those who learned it from the children of their slave ancestors.

Lawrence McKiver has been able to function as a pivotal and influential folk artist because his life and his self-awareness have been profoundly informed not only by an inherited culture shaped by the folkways of the African diaspora, slavery, and the religion and agrarian way of life of his forebears, but also by the fact that he has been an alert and creative participant in changing times. The passion and strength he brings to his artistic voice are matters of choice; steeped as he is in traditional ways and beliefs, he is not a marginal survivor on some isolated, imagined or real "Gullah island" where physical isolation and lack of alternative choices allowed for the continuation of the ancient slave ring shout and allied traditions in earlier forms. Indeed, we have seen that the southeastern ring shout survived the longest in a mainland community. Lawrence is very much a man of the mainland— he has said that he would never wish to live on an island like Sapelo and has been uncomfortable the few times he has been there, preferring instead to be able to get in his car, get on the highway, and go "somewhere." Even in his youth, he was, within the limits of his means and his location, in some ways a young man of the jazz age, a "sport" with up-to-date clothes and a "piece of a car," listening to newer imported musical sounds and dancing new steps in clubs and juke joints—even as he was retaining the deep religious faith of his ancestors and singing their shout songs. In his later years, as a septuagenarian on stage at the Black Arts Festival in Atlanta's Piedmont Park singing to a multiracial audience or sitting alone in his house composing new songs that address the problems of youth in his community, Lawrence McKiver provides a model for a way in which a deeply sensitive and gifted folk artist can adapt ancient traditions for new times.

4 | The Shout Songs

Along with the shout itself, the shouters of Bolden have preserved a sizeable and impressive repertoire of shout songs. These are today considered a distinct category of song, used only in conjunction with the shout and related percussion. The shout songs would never be sung in church in place of spirituals, hymns, or gospel songs of recent vintage—nor would these serve the needs of the shout. We have seen that in an earlier time there was some overlapping of the shout songs or "runnin' spirituals" and other spirituals, and clearly the shout songs have influenced later religious—and secular— African American musical forms. Rowing songs and work songs that have passed from use had similar call-and-response patterns: a field-work song, such as "The Grey Goose" that John and Alan Lomax recorded in Texas prisons, is a secular narrative cousin of the shout songs and very close in structure. Call-and-response forms akin to the shout songs are common in modern gospel singing. The shout songs are richly varied musically and in their texts and mood. The melodies and rhythms hint at the richness of antebellum black folk songs and fuse African and European American elements. It is easy to see why some of the shout songs struck outsiders as repetitious chants when compared with the melodic lyricism of early spirituals; yet many of the shout songs, such as "Army, Cross Over," have stirringly beautiful melodies. The texts, along with the dramatic shouts they accompany, range in expressive mood from playful to fervently apocalyptic. Many of the shout songs we have recorded in Bolden have been collected, in other variants, along the southeastern coast and beyond; several have not been recovered previously. Though there was unquestionably a degree of exposure to shout song traditions in neighboring communities in the post-Emancipation years, it is clear from the testimony of today's Bolden shouters that the bulk of their songs were passed down to them in a strong family-community tradition, from slaves on the Wylly and Hopkins plantations largely through London and Amy Jenkins. This slave-born couple were certainly prodigious singers and shouters.

There is an active and an inactive repertoire of shout songs. Years ago all the songs were used in the shout, but now fewer are sung and shouted to at Watch Night and in public performances. "Blow, Gabriel," "Move, Daniel," "Eve and Adam," and several others are perennial favorites, and "Farewell, Last Day Goin'" is always sung at the conclusion of the Watch Night shout. Lawrence McKiver cannot get his basers to provide the correct background for others, and they have fallen into disuse; he has been willing to record these, doing the difficult task of providing both call and response. Some songs were the "property" of a particular songster; "Wade the Water to My Knees" was Sister Lucille Holloway's song, and after she died no one cared to sing it at the shout. Lawrence knows all the shout songs but will not sing that one: "I *can* sing it, but I can't sing it like her . . . she got a voice for that song . . . that song go with a *pitiful* voice, I say not a *pitiful* voice, but a *touching* voice," clarifying that that song is best sung by someone with an alto or soprano voice. Likewise Lawrence recalls "I Come to Tell You" as his mother's "special song" but adds that his "basers can't master all the songs I can sing." Nonetheless, as recently as the summer of 1994, Lawrence McKiver has rehearsed his singers in some of the less-used shout songs and performed them for the public, thus renewing them in practice.

The shout songs create joy and spiritual release in the participants, as does the shout, but the songs never cause people to "shout" in the sense of becoming so overwhelmed that they "fall out," as spirituals and hymns in the church can. According to McKiver,

> Not in the ring shout, I never have seen them [fall out]. But I have
> seen the preacher be singing, and different strong choirs that touched

some people, they fall out . . . [but] no, no, no, no, I never did see one to fall out in the ring shout. Never did. They be happy. But I never have seen one be happy enough to fall out in the ring shout in all my days. Never have. They shout, shout, shout round, and if one maybe get tired, they stand up side the wall and the other one come in and shout, shout, shout. They were sincere in what they doing. . . . The shout songs is a happy thing, you ever paying attention. I don't believe they be thinking about what the past was. . . . They enjoying them-selves, they come from where they work, they done store away their little stuff like that, and just going do that shout. It was just a happy thing around the old folks. And the young . . ." [Comments above are from our interview, February 12, 1994.]

Here, then, are the shout songs of Bolden as sung by Lawrence McKiver and other songsters and basers. These twenty-five songs are the largest number of shout songs to be published since *Slave Songs of the United States,* which appeared during the heyday of the shout in the last century. That this quantity and quality of shout songs could be recovered at this late date is a tribute to the retentive memories and the will to sustain the tradition of the songsters of Bolden, especially the finest of them all, Lawrence McKiver. Transcriptions from recorded performances, all of which were recorded by the author in the field or in stage performances, will provide the texts, melodies, and rhythmic accompaniments of the leaders, basers, stickers, and clappers. Each transcription will describe a specific performance rather than collate more than one; occasionally, alternate texts and musical variations from other performances will be given. When a dis-tinctive shout is performed to a certain song, it will be described as well, along with the meaning and background of the songs and shouts as given by the informants and found in comparative references.

Jubilee

Sung by Lawrence McKiver and group, St. Simons Island, August 20, 1983 (Folkways Records FE 4344).

McKiver says that this song was sung and shouted when the slaves were emancipated. It has long been understood that slave songs frequently carried a double message of spiritual release and of hope for—or the re-joicing in—liberation from slavery in this world; both of these meanings are amply clear in this song. The bitter reference to the slaves being considered Christians on Sunday and devils on Monday by their masters is offset by the triumphant line "shout my children, 'cause you're free," suggesting that the shout itself was a celebration of freedom. Parrish gives a similar shout song, "My Soul Rock on Jubilee" (p. 89). The percussive pattern of the sticker and clappers is given here in full below the vocal parts. Subsequently, for reasons of space, this standard percussive pattern will be indicated by an asterisk (*) where it commences, except in cases where there are variations in the percussion; in these instances the percussion will be provided.

Leader:

Jubilee, jubilee

Basers:

Oh, my lord

Leader:

Jubilee in the mornin'

Basers:

My Lord, jubilee!

Jubilee in the evenin' / Jubilee in the mornin' /
Jubilee, jubilee / Jubilee, jubilee /
Walkin', members, walkin' / Walkin' on yo' Jesus /
Shout my children, 'cause yo' free! / My God brought you liberty /
Call me a Sunday Christian / Call me a Monday devil /
Don' care what you call me / So long Jesus love me /
Jubilee, jubilee / Jubilee, jubilee /
Jubilee, jubilee / Jubilee, jubilee /
Walkin', members, walkin' / Walkin' on yo' Jesus /
Shout, my children, 'cause yo' free / My God brought you liberty /
Jubilee, jubilee / Jubilee in the mornin' /
Jubilee in the evenin' / Jubilee in the mornin' /
Call me a Sunday Christian / Call me a Monday devil /
Don' care what you call me / So long Jesus love me /

Jubilee

Blow, Gabriel

Sung by Lawrence McKiver and group, St. Simons Island, August 20, 1983. This recording can be heard on *McIntosh County Shouters: Slave Shout Songs from the Coast of Georgia* (Folkways Records FE 4344).

In this energetic shout song, the singer exhorts the Archangel Gabriel to blow his trumpet on the Day of Judgement; it may be the antecedent of later spirituals on this theme or may have developed parallel to them. Parrish (pp. 87–88) gives a similar version she collected on St. Simons Island. In the 1970s Mary Arnold Twining collected "Blow, Gabriel" on St. Simons as it was performed by the Georgia Sea Island Singers and identifies it as a "shout song" (Twining, *An Examination of African Retentions in the Folk Culture of the South Carolina and Georgia Sea Islands* [Indiana University, Ph.D. diss., 1977, p. 89]). There are two spirituals on the same theme in *Slave Songs of the United States.* "Blow Your Trumpet, Gabriel" was collected by Charles Pickard Ware on Port Royal and by Mrs. C. W. Bowen in Charleston. Odum and Johnson (*The Negro and His Songs,* pp. 86–87) include "Blow, Gable." Also, see above, in chapter 1, Charlotte Forten's description of Georgia blind slave, Maurice, singing "Gabriel Blow the Trumpet" (Joyner, *Folk Song in South Carolina,* p. 44). In the documented performance that follows, the singing drops off and a percussive interlude of stick beating and hand clapping is heard. In this and following transcriptions a slash (/) will indicate the basers' responses, in this case alternating "judgement" and "judgement bar."

Leader:

Blow, Gabriel!

Basers:

Judgement!

Leader:

Blow that trumpet!

Basers:

Judgement bar!

Blow, Gabriel

Calm and easy / Tell everybody /
My God say / That they got to meet /
Oh blow, Gabriel / Blow that trumpet /
Louder and louder / Got to wake my people /
Wherever they be / On lan' or sea /
Tell everybody / My God say /
That they got to be / Blow, Gabriel /
Blow that trumpet / Louder and louder /
Gon' see my mother / My father, too /
Blow, Gabriel / Oh blow your trumpet /
Louder an' louder / Tell everybody /
That they got to meet / They got to meet /
Blow, Gabriel / Blow, Gabriel /
Calm an' easy / Wake my people /
Wherever they be / On lan' or sea /
Blow, Gabriel / Gon' see my mother /
An' my father, too / Oh, blow, Gabriel /
Oh, blow yo' trumpet / Blow yo' trumpet /
Wake my people / Wherever they be /
On lan' or sea / Tell 'em I say /
My God say / That they got to be— /
Oh, blow, Gabriel / Blow your trumpet /
Louder an' louder / Wake my people /
Wherever they be / On lan' or sea /
Oh, blow, Gabriel / Blow your trumpet /
See my mother / An' my father, too /
Blow, Gabriel / Blow your trumpet /
Louder an' louder / Blow that trumpet /
Wake my people / Wherever they be
On lan' or sea / Blow, Gabriel /
(similarly, until end)

Move for Your Dyin' Savior

Sung by Lawrence McKiver, Bolden, February 12, 1994.

This is a shout song that McKiver had forgotten for a long time, and after singing it, he reflected on how he recalled it: "And just keep on like that, words after words. That song was goin' out of my rememberance, and one of my sister, sister that sing so well, say, 'Lawrence, you ever sing that song "Move for Your Dyin' Savior,"' and I take the song back into my mind. And I rehearse it a little bit. I'm something like a mockingbird, I sings everybody's tune but mine. A mockingbird sings all the birds' tune, but he never have a special song of his own. I be mocking all them songs, spirituals, shout songs, solos, different stuff. That's the things I like to do."

Move, children, move
   Move for your dyin' Savior
Shout, children, shout
   Shout for your dyin' Savior
Seekin', seekin'
   Seek for your dyin' Savior
Sing, sing
   Sing for my dyin' Savior

I'm lookin', lookin'
   For my dyin' Savior
I'm prayin', prayin'
   For my dyin' Savior

Move for Your Dyin' Savior

I Want to Die Like Weepin' Mary

Sung by Lucille Holloway and group, Bolden, September 5, 1981 (Folkways Records FE 4344).

Lucille Holloway was born in 1910 and died in 1982. First cousin to Lawrence McKiver, Odessa Young, and Oneitha Ellison, and cousin to Catherine Campbell, she was a faithful church member and an adherent to the old-time shouting tradition. In 1981 she told me, "The old-time way, that's the best way. If you come up then, you would say so, too. . . . Modern time making your heart bleed. Modern times is the devil." Catherine Campbell said she was one of the best to "set" the songs—that is, start appropriately slow and with proper concentration, and pick up the correct tempo called for by the shout. Lucille Holloway put it this way: "I don't lead all the songs, but them what I lead, if they turn it loose to me, I can set it so you can shout. You can't drag a song." This song has not been reported previously in this form, but it may be derived from the shape-note song "Weeping Mary" (see George Pullen Jackson, *White Spirituals in the Southern Uplands*, pp. 255–56).

Leader:

 I want to die like weepin' Mary

Basers:

 Sit 'side, side of my Jesus

Leader:

 I want to die like weepin' Mary

Basers:

 Sit 'side, side of my Jesus

Leader:

 Sit yo' side

Basers:

 'Side of my Jesus

(similarly)

Side by side / Sit yo' side /
Anyway / Anyway /
Sit yo' side / Sit yo' side /
Side by side / Side by side /
Oh Lord / Oh Lord /

Anyway / Anyway /
Anyway / Side by side /
Oh, Lord / Oh, Lord

I Want to Die Like Weepin' Mary

Wade the Water to My Knees

Sung by Lucille Holloway and group, Bolden, September 5, 1981 (Folkways Records FE 4344).

Like the previous song, this shout song confronts the inevitability of death. Unlike "I Want to Die Like Weepin' Mary" however, it does not picture meeting Jesus "on the other side," but rather the terror of dying is seen as wading into cold water, a metaphor occurring in numerous spirituals. Sister Holloway was a wonderfully able traditional singer. She added intensity and excitement to shout songs she led by continually introducing melodic and rhythmic variations to the leader's vocal line, here notated in detail.

Leader:
> I wade the water to my knees

Basers:
> I'm gon' pray, gon' pray

Leader:
> Wade the water to my knees

Basers:
> I'm gon' pray till I die

(similarly)
Lord, the water's so cold / Lord, the water's so cold /
I'm gon' sink an' never rise / I'm gon' sink an' never rise /
Oh, Lord, have mercy! / Oh, Lord, have mercy /
Oh, Lord, have mercy / Oh, Lord, have mercy /
Oh the water's so cold / Oh the water's so cold /
Oh, Lord, have mercy / Oh, Lord, have mercy /

Wade the Water to My Knees

Army Cross Over

Sung by Lawrence McKiver, Bolden, May 18, 1992.

McKiver calls this one of his sister's songs. He explained the genesis of the song: "Some of the songs bracket off from the Bible, such as 'Joshuay, my army cross over,' *touching* words from the Bible, and they make the song" (interview, February 12, 1994). On the present recording he sings both the leader and the basers parts, saying, "I'm doing double, I'm trying to do my basers, and switch back to my lead, and that's uncomfortable." This is because the call and the response do not simply alternate, they overlap, as Allen noted early on. Yet McKiver succeeds in giving a serviceable rendering of the song and provides many variations on the melody, notated here. Allen gives two versions of this song: one he collected in Port Royal, another from "Col. Higginson's regiment," is said to be from Sapelo Island, Georgia. There was an association with imagery of biblical and worldly armies during the time of the Civil War; the version from Higginson's freedmen troops refers to Pharaoh's army, McKiver's to Joshua's army, though he refers to the Red Sea.

Leader:
    My army, my army
Basers:
    Army cross over
Leader:
    This is Joshuay's soldier
Basers:
    Army cross over

Yes, my army, army
    Army cross over
We cross that mighty Red Sea,
    Army cross over.

We fight that mighty battle
    Army cross over
We never lose a battle,
    Army cross over.

Joshuay pray to God to stop the sun
    Army cross over
Until this battle he has won,
    Army cross over.

Oh, my army, my army
    Army cross over
Joshuay's army,
    Army cross over.

Army Cross Over

Happy Angel

Sung by Lawrence McKiver, Bolden, February 12, 1994.

McKiver learned this old shout song, which was sometimes used at the conclusion of the Watch Night shout, from his sister Gussie. This song is not in the active repertoire of the Bolden shouters. Lawrence sang it in the course of an interview in his home, providing both the leader's calls and the basers' refrains. Lydia Parrish documents a version called "Ha'k 'E Angels," which she collected from Deacon Eddy Thorpe of McIntosh County; Thorpe "explained that the slaves, when allowed to go to a praise house that was out of bounds, were given passes with their promise to return before sun-up. On New Year's Eve the service consisted of prayers, religious songs, and a sermon by the preacher. At midnight, different members offered thanks to the good Lord for the blessings of the past twelve months and implored His aid for the year to come. The shouting then began, and continued until dawn" (Parrish, pp. 56–61). This could describe present-day Watch Nights in Bolden, except that nowadays the shouting is in the annex of the church rather than in a praise house, and the shout winds down before dawn.

Happy angel
  Day's a-comin'
Happy angel
  Day's a-comin'
Look out the window
  I see day

Happy angel
  Day's a-comin'
Day, oh day
  I see day
Happy angel
  Day's a-comin'
Look out the window

(spoken)
Different ones sing
(sung)
Happy angel
  Change my name
Change my name for the comin' day
Happy angel
  Change my name

Happy Angel

♩=92

Hap-py an-gel,___ Day's a-com-in',___ Hap-py an-gel,___ Day's a-com-in'___

Look out the win-dow,___ I see day,___ Hap-py an-gel,___ Day's a-com-in'___

Day,___ oh day   I see day

Move, Daniel

Sung by Lawrence McKiver with group. St. Simons Island, August 21, 1983 (Folkways Records FE 4344).

This song accompanies one of the most active and widespread of the shouts. The religious content of the refrain suggests that the song has a sacred message, and a listener might assume that the Daniel referred to is the biblical prophet. But Lawrence McKiver states explicitly that the Daniel is "not the Daniel in the Bible," but rather a slave who, having stolen some meat, is fleeing the master's whip. The shout becomes a dramatic symbolic expression of solidarity between Daniel and his fellow slaves, as they instruct him to move, turn the other way, and in a beautiful gesture of arms extended birdlike from the shoulders, "do the eagle wing" as he evades the master (we have noted in chapter 2 that this gesture, while having precedent in earlier practice of the shout in Bolden, has been exaggerated in the interest of "showmanship" by the McIntosh County Shouters, and that it has reentered community practice in this form). The sensual rocking motion of the hips at the command, "rock, Daniel, rock," was noted by Robert Gordon (Gordon, "The Negro Spiritual" in *Carolina Low Country,* p. 201) and was likely another form of self-assertion disguised as dancelike play. Hidden messages carrying protests against slavery and jokes on the master eluded earlier white observers including Lydia Parrish, who commented about how southern blacks did not volunteer information (Parrish, p. 20). In his foreword to the 1965 edition of Parrish's book, Bruce Jackson criticized her paternalistic assumption: "She doesn't realize that the slave and former slave might have been loath to offer the white southern plantation owner or manager information for the same reason a convict does not chat freely with the warden or a union organizer with company lawyer" (Parrish, 1965, pp. vii–viii). It is possible that McKiver's and the Bolden shouters' understanding of the song may not be the "original" sense, but, as one commentator has suggested, "a story grafted on to a pre-existing song." Johann Buis observes: "A moderate tempo camouflages the steady navigational clues for the surreptitious act which this song portrays. . . . Akin, in some ways to the square dance caller, who keeps the musical flow, while at the same time supplying verbal cues for motion in process, the leader here was intended to show his improvisatory skills as a musical strategist, while exhibiting a remarkable performance craft. To simply regard this song as pantomimic would ignore the high degree of performance sophistication which the original creation of the song called for." Bessie Jones and Bess Lomax Hawes cite "Daniel" as a shout, with tune, text, and detailed descriptions of the shout steps and movements that are very similar to the McIntosh County version; there is no reference to secular meanings (Jones and Hawes, *Step It Down*, pp. 143–45). The song, as led by Willis Proctor and a group from the Georgia Sea Island Singers and recorded by Alan Lomax, was released on *Georgia Sea Islands, Volume I* (Prestige International LP 25001). Mary Arnold Twining later collected the song from John Davis of St. Simons, a member of the Georgia Sea Island Singers; he was accompanied by his brother Peter who beat a cane, curved end down, in rhythm along with singers. Davis included the "kneebone bend" among the movements called for, but Twining does not give any meaning Davis may have attached to the song (Twining, *An Examination of African Retentions in the Folk Culture of the South Carolina and Georgia Sea Islands*, Indiana University, Ph.D. diss., 1977, pp. 72–73). Lawrence McKiver is clear enough about his understanding of the meaning of this shout in his spoken introduction to its performance: "I want to sing a song about 'Move, Daniel.' See, Daniel was a slave, and the slaves all were havin' a little party across the field one day. And the smoke-house was up there—we call it the smoke-house, the place that the old boss keep all his meat. And they wanted to steal some of the meat, you know, and they send Daniel in to get a piece of meat so they could put the party on sure enough! And old boss was coming down through there, so the slaves going to sing a song to let Daniel know to get out the way. 'Cause Daniel could pick it up and put it down! You know, I mean that fast run, that's what I'm talking about. So old boss thought they was singing a party song, but they was telling Daniel how to get out the way, so that old boss wouldn't put that whip-lash on him. So I'm goin' to sing the song—I jus' want to let you all know why we sing the song 'Move, Daniel.'"

Leader:
> Move, Daniel, move, Daniel,
> Move, Daniel, move

Basers:
> Daniel.

Leader:
> Move, Daniel, move

Basers:
> Daniel.

Chorus (leader and basers):
> Oh, Lord, pray sinner, come,
> Oh, Lord, sinner gone to hell.

Move, Daniel

(similarly)
Move, Daniel, move, Daniel
Move, Daniel, move, Daniel.

Go the other way, Daniel
Go the other way, Daniel.

Rock, Daniel, rock, Daniel
Rock, Daniel, rock, Daniel.

Shout, Daniel, shout, Daniel
Shout, Daniel, shout, Daniel.

(chorus)
Move, Daniel, move, Daniel
Move, Daniel, move, Daniel.

Go the other way, Daniel
Go the other way, Daniel.

Sinner in the way, Lord
Sinner in the way, Lord.

(chorus)
Move, Daniel, move, Daniel
Move, Daniel, move, Daniel.

Shout, Daniel, shout, Daniel
Shout, Daniel, shout, Daniel.

Rock, Daniel, rock, Daniel
Rock, Daniel, rock, Daniel.

Go the other way, Daniel
Go the other way, Daniel.

Sinner in my way, Lord
Sinner in my way, Lord.

Move, Daniel, move, Daniel
Move, Daniel, move, Daniel.

(chorus)
Move, Daniel, move, Daniel
Move, Daniel, move, Daniel.

Do the eagle wing, Daniel
Do the eagle wing, Daniel.

Shout, Daniel, shout, Daniel
Shout, Daniel, shout, Daniel.

Rock, Daniel, rock, Daniel
Rock, Daniel, rock, Daniel.

(chorus)
(continue ad lib)

Drive Ol' Joe

Sung by Lawrence McKiver, Bolden, July 29, 1994.

"Drive Ol' Joe" is not in the active Bolden repertoire, and again Lawrence McKiver sang both the leader's calls and the basers' responses, including an alternative refrain ("Oh Lord, drive 'im"). This song makes direct reference to slavery and to Joe, a slave who was a traitor to his fellow slaves, as McKiver described in his narrative accompanying his singing of the song; he also described the dramatic pantomine that was part of this shout as he saw it performed during his boyhood by his mother and aunts: "That's a song was sung by the slaves, they tell me. Joe was a guy—we call him a 'cheese eater,' he would tell the old slave master every thing that the slaves do, stay on the good side . . . of the slave master. And the slaves didn't like him, you see. They didn't want him around. See, the slave' would steal from they master, anything they could get, and John go an' tell the owner. So therefore they didn't want him. That's the way the song was established from. They would say, 'Drive ol' Joe, drive 'im from the window / Drive 'im from the do' / He cheat my father's children.' [When the old sisters did this shout] they be throwing up their hands, they have a handkerchief, 'drive 'im from the window, drive 'im from the do'.' I had an auntie could really sing that song. Her name was Sarah Jackson. She was a Jenkins, after she married she was a Jackson. She really could sing that song."

Drive ol' Joe	Drive 'im
Drive 'im	Don't want 'im roun' us
Drive 'im from the window	Drive 'im
Drive 'im	(spoken)
Drive 'im from the do'	The background say
Drive 'im	(sung)
Drive ol' Joe	Oh Lord, drive 'im

Drive Ol' Joe

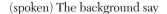

I Come to Tell You

I Come to Tell You

Sung by Lawrence McKiver in Bolden, February 12, 1994.

This shout song was the "special song" of McKiver's mother, Charlotte Evans.

I come to tell you—where my God send me
To preach a sermon—in Jerusalem
And I got to go—wherever He send me
I got the hymn book—and I got my Bible
Gon' tell all the nation—that my God send me
Some gonna believe me—some gonna deceive me
But I mus' go—wherever He send me
Tell me not to worry—'cause He'll be with me
Jus' open my mouth—and He'll speak for me
Spread good tidings—He will defend me

Kneebone Bend

Sung by Doretha Skipper and group, Bolden, December 17, 1983 (Folkways Records FE 4344).

The shouters of Bolden consider this the oldest shout song—sung and shouted by their ancestors when they arrived from Africa and bent their knees in prayer. Parrish, who agrees that this is one "of the more primitive Afro-American chants," says that the song was used for rowing, and provides a line of "the rowing version [which] calls for 'knee-bone bend to the elbow bend'" (Parrish, p. 80). When the shouters of Bolden perform this, they not only bend their knees at the command, but they incorporate a hesitation in the movement, which McKiver calls a "catch-it." Here the basers do not sing the responses in unison but employ harmony, in this case fifths. Alan Lomax recorded a very similar version from the Georgia Sea Island Singers in 1959 (Prestige International LP 25001; reissued on New World NW-278).

Kneebone Bend

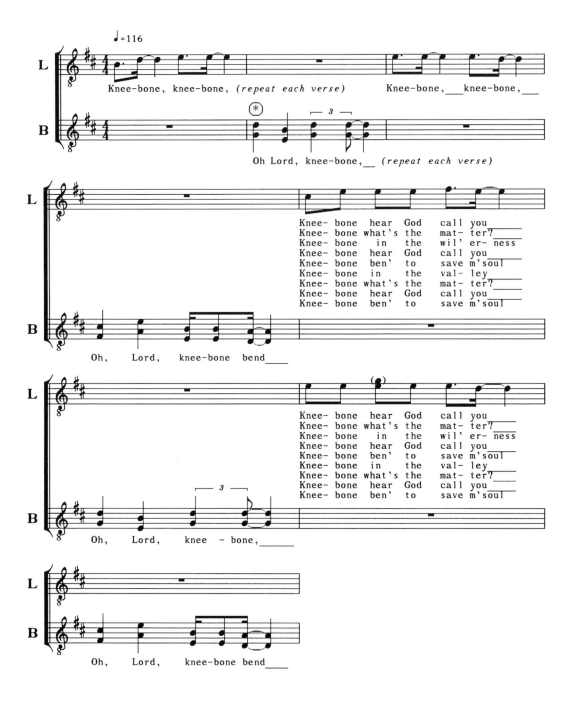

Leader:
    Kneebone, kneebone
Basers:
    Oh, Lord, kneebone
Leader:
    Kneebone, kneebone
Basers:
    Oh, Lord, kneebone bend.

(similarly)
Kneebone hear God call you
    Oh, Lord, kneebone
Kneebone hear God call you
    Oh, Lord, kneebone bend.

Kneebone, kneebone
    Oh, Lord, kneebone
Kneebone, kneebone
    Oh, Lord, kneebone bend.

Kneebone, what's the matter?
    Oh, Lord, kneebone.
Kneebone, what's the matter?
    Oh, Lord, kneebone bend.

Kneebone, kneebone
    Oh, Lord, kneebone
Kneebone, kneebone
    Oh, Lord, kneebone bend.

Kneebone in the wil'erness
    Oh, Lord, kneebone
Kneebone in the wil'erness
    Oh, Lord, kneebone bend.

Kneebone, hear God call you
    Oh, Lord, kneebone
Kneebone, hear God call you
    Oh, Lord, kneebone bend.

Kneebone, kneebone
    Oh, Lord, kneebone
Kneebone, kneebone
    Oh, Lord, kneebone bend.

Kneebone ben' to save m' soul
    Oh, Lord, kneebone
Kneebone ben' to save m' soul
    Oh, Lord, kneebone bend.

Kneebone in the valley
    Oh, Lord, kneebone
Kneebone in the valley
    Oh, Lord, kneebone bend.

Kneebone, kneebone
    Oh, Lord, kneebone
Kneebone, kneebone
    Oh, Lord, kneebone bend.

Kneebone, what's the matter?
    Oh, Lord, kneebone
Kneebone, what's the matter?
    Oh, Lord, kneebone bend.

(continue ad lib)

Pharaoh's Host Got Lost

Pharaoh's Host Got Lost

Sung by Lawrence McKiver and group, Bolden, September 5, 1981
(Folkways Records FE 4344).

This shout song moves on a fine minor melody that is related to that of the famous spiritual on the same subject, "Go, Down, Moses"; the concluding line of the present song, "in that Red Sea," is identical in melody to the concluding "let my people go" in the spiritual. For a related song, see "Didn't Old Pharaoh Get Lost" (James Weldon Johnson, *The Book of American Negro Spirituals*, pp. 60–61). Johann Buis offers an analysis of the song and its performance by the Bolden shouters: "In the tradition of the Hebrew concept of *zachor*, remembrance, this very interactive call-and-response reminds all participants that beyond the action of Moses laying down his rod and pharaoh's host, is the One who orchestrated the event (though the word God never appears). The irregular rhythmic clapping of the group suggests the obvious galloping of horses (even in the singing the linguistic barrier between 'horse' and 'host' is blurred significantly). Moreover, the irregularity of the clapping hints at aurally portraying the befuddled cavalry. This irregular (polyrhythmic) aural portrayal uses rhythmic sophistication in a way Western Renaissance and Baroque composers used text-painting to melodically portray tangible and intangible objects and concepts."

Leader:

    Moses, Moses, lay your rod

Leader and basers:

    In that Red Sea

Leader:

    Lay your rod, let the children cross

Leader and Basers:

    In that Red Sea.

Chorus:

    Ol' Pharaoh's hos' got los', los', los',
    Ol' Pharaoh's hos' got los',
      In that Red Sea.
    They shout when the hos' got los', los', los',
    They shout when the hos' got los',
      In that Red Sea.

Leader:

> Moses, Moses, lay your rod

Leader and basers:

> In that Red Sea

Leader:

> Lay your rod, let the children cross

Leader and basers:

> In that Red Sea.

Chorus:

> Ol' Pharaoh's hos' got los', los', los'
> Pharaoh's hos' got los',
>> In that Red Sea.

Leader:

> Oh Moses, please lay your rod

Leader and basers:

> In that Red Sea

Leader:

> Lay your rod, let the children cross

Leader and basers:

> In that Red Sea.

Chorus:

> Ol' Pharaoh's hos' got los', los', los'
> Pharaoh's hos' got los', los', los'
> Such a weepin' when the hos' got los'
>> In that Red Sea.

Hold the Baby

Sung by Doretha Skipper and group, Bolden, December 17, 1983 (Folkways Records FE 4344).

This is one of the few entirely secular shout songs. According to Lawrence McKiver, who agreed that while the song was not about religion, it was "about life": "How my mamma explain it to me, my aunties and surrounding ladies, explain it to me like this, that the man and his wife—the man was working, he come in, he was tired, and the baby was crying, and the wife wanted the husband to hold the baby, and he was telling her to hold the baby, take possession of the baby, 'cause he was tired, he had to go to work the next day, and he wanted to get him some rest, and that's where the

song was made up from . . . the baby crying, need some medicine, need a
doctor, need some water, put that in there, and join up a song." McKiver's
text is much like Doretha Skipper's; Skipper learned it from her mother,
Fannie Palmer.

Leader: Oh what's the matter? /
    Hol' the baby   Oh mama's baby /
Basers: Oh he need some water /
    Hol' 'im   Oh rock the baby /
Leader: Oh he need some medicine /
    Hol' the baby   Oh he got the fever /
Basers: Oh rock the baby /
    Hol' 'im   Oh he got the fever /
Leader: Oh he need the doctor /
    Hol' the baby   Oh rock the baby /
Basers: Oh mama' baby /
    Oh, ho' the mam' ba'.   Oh want some water /
                                                 Oh he need some medicine /
(similarly)   Oh he need the doctor /
                                                 Oh he got the fever /

Hold the Baby

Religion, So Sweet

Sung by Lawrence McKiver and group, St. Simons Island, August 20, 1984 (Folkways Records FE 4344).

McKiver usually precedes the performance of this shout, one of the more light-spirited ones, with a skit in which he assumes the high voice of a woman, and the shouters assume the roles of her children assembled to sing and shout this song for her birthday. Such a shout as this can go on for some time, with the leader improvising on a few recurring couplets. We give a lengthy text of a typical performance here to illustrate how Lawrence McKiver adds interest by adeptly varying and repeating the stock lines of the shout song. Gordon gives the text of a related song to illustrate a verse and chorus style of ring shout: "Oh we'll walk around the fountain" being the slower verse, and a repeated "Oh religion, oh religion, oh religion, so sweet!" being the faster chorus (Gordon, "The Negro Spiritual" in *The Carolina Low Country*, pp. 199–200). Charles Pickard Ware collected a version, "Religion So Sweet," on Port Royal Island in the 1860s (*Slave Songs of the United States*, p. 13).

Leader:

    Oh, that 'ligion

Basers:

    So sweet

Leader:

    Eh, Lord,

Basers:

    So sweet.

(similarly)

Now shout the 'ligion, So sweet
Now sing the 'ligion, So sweet

It made me happy, So sweet
Early one mornin', So sweet

I shout the 'ligion, So sweet
I talk about the 'ligion, So sweet

I sing about the 'ligion, So sweet
It made me happy, So sweet

Early one mornin', So sweet
I tell ever'body, So sweet

About the 'ligion, So sweet
Eh, Lord, So sweet

Now sing yo' 'ligion, So sweet
Now shout yo' 'ligion, So Sweet

It made me happy, So sweet
Early one mornin', So sweet

I tell ever'body, So sweet
About the 'ligion, so sweet

I sing the 'ligion, So sweet
I shout the 'ligion, So sweet

It made me happy, So sweet
Early one mornin', So sweet

I shout the 'ligion, So sweet
I sing the 'ligion, So sweet

I telled everybody, So sweet
About the 'ligion, So sweet

Oh, that 'ligion, So sweet
Oh that 'ligion, So sweet

Made me happy, So sweet
Early one mornin', So sweet

I rock the 'ligion, So sweet
I rock the 'ligion, So sweet

I sing the 'ligion, So sweet
'Cause it made me happy, So sweet

I sing the 'ligion, So sweet
'Cause it made me happy, So sweet

Early one mornin', So sweet
I telled ever'body, So sweet

About the 'ligion, So sweet
Oh, Lord, So sweet

Oh that 'ligion, So sweet
Eh, child, So sweet

Now sing you' 'ligion, So sweet
Now sing that 'ligion, So sweet

Now shout that 'ligion, So sweet
Now rock that 'ligion, So sweet

Eh, child, So sweet
Ah, child, So sweet

It made me happy, So sweet
So happy, So sweet

It made me happy, So sweet
I telled ever'body, So sweet

About my 'ligion, So sweet
I sing my 'ligion, So sweet

Now shout the 'ligion, So sweet
Eh, Lord, So sweet

Oh that 'ligion, So sweet
Shout that 'ligion, So sweet

Shout that 'ligion, So sweet
Shout yo' 'ligion, So sweet

Now rock the 'ligion, So sweet
Now rock the 'ligion, So sweet

Now rock that 'ligion, So sweet
Oh, yeah, So sweet

Made me happy, So sweet
Early one mornin', so sweet

Sing yo' 'ligion, So sweet
Now rock the 'ligion, So sweet

Now rock that 'ligion . . .

Religion, So Sweet

Time Drawin' Nigh (I See the Sign)

Sung by Rev. Nathan Palmer and group, Bolden, January 1, 1982 (Folkways Records FE 4434).

This is one of the most impressive and dramatic of the shout songs. Parrish gives a version from St. Simons Island, "Ay Lord, Time Is Drawin' Nigh," with a refrain, "hmmmh," that she says is "sung by the basers with closed lips. This odd nasal tone adds attractive variety to a fine piece of melodic construction." She gives a McIntosh County text as well, related to the one sung in Bolden today, with the comment that "none but a Negro poet could have created the imagery of the . . . lines" (Parrish, pp. 185–88). On Watch Night 1982 Reverend Palmer was persuaded to sing this by participants who admired his ability as a songster, and who realized that he was no longer active as a leader: "Rev', you want to sing us a song? One. One. Please, one, for the New Year, one . . . yeah, he'll do it, he'll do it." His text is given, followed by a fuller text as led by Lawrence McKiver and Freddie Palmer.

Leader:		(similarly)
	Horse in the valley	Oh, who's gonna ride 'im /
Basers:		Oh, look over yonder /
	Hey!	Sun refused to shine /
Leader:		Oh tell me what's the matter /
	Horse in the valley	Oh, Judgement Day! /
Basers:		Oh run to the rock /
	Hey!	It's no hidin' place /
Leader:		Oh, an' the rock cried out /
	Horse in the valley	I can't hide myself /
Basers:		Oh look over yonder /
	Hey, Lord, time drawin' nigh!	Oh two tall angels /
		Jus' standin' at the Judgement /
		(spoken)
		Hey, he could do it!

Time Drawin' Nigh (I See the Sign)

Second variant, sung by Lawrence McKiver and Freddie Palmer (leaders) and group, Morton Theater, Athens, Georgia, June 25, 1994.

Leader (McKiver):
> I see the sign

Basers:
> Hey

Leader:
> I see the sign

Basers:
> Hey

Leader:
> I see the sign

Basers:
> Hey, Lord, time drawin' nigh.

(similarly)
Sign of the Judgement /
Sign in the fig tree /
Loose horse in the valley /
Tell me who's gon' ride 'im /

King Jesus is the rider /
Sinner, come out the corner /
Tell me what you gonna do /
Where you runnin', sinner? /
Sinner run to the rock /
No hidin' place /
Rock cried out /
It's Judgement day! /
No hidin' place /
Can't hide myself /

Leaders (McKiver and Palmer):
      Two tall angels /
      On the chariot wheel /
      They talkin' 'bout the Judgement /
Leader (McKiver):
      Look over yonder /
      Dark cloud risin' /
Leaders (McKiver and Palmer):
      The sun won't shine /
      Sinner come out the corner /
Leader (Palmer):
      Loose horse in the valley /
      Who's gonna ride 'im? /
      King Jesus gonna ride 'im /
      Rock cried out /
      Can't hide myself! /

Read 'em, John

Sung by Lawrence McKiver and group, Bolden, December 17, 1983
(Folkways Records FE 4344). A similar performance of this song by the
Georgia Sea Island Singers can be heard on Prestige-International
LP 25001, reissued on New World 278.

The catchy melody of this shout song is very similar to that of the
slavery-days banjo reel "Johnny Booker." McKiver claims that the song relates to the Emancipation, and the slaves had to trust one among them who

could read to tell them they really were free. Any slave with such knowledge had to have gained it surreptitiously. According to one white who grew up on a McIntosh County Plantation, "As to teaching them [slaves] to read and write, 'Self-preservation is the first law of nature,' and the country was so flooded with abolition literature that the slave-owner felt his only safety lay in keeping the Negroes ignorant" (Georgia Bryan Conrad, *Reminiscences of a Southern Woman* [n.d.], p. 14). McKiver explains, "This song—when they was comin' out of slave', none of 'em could read, but John, he around the kitchen a little bit, and he learned to read a little. So they had a letter to tell 'em they was free, but they didn't believe it, so they ask John to read the letter, and this is the way it went."

Leader:

> John brought the letter,
> Laid it on the table,
> Tell all the members read 'em, oh
> Read 'em, let me go.
>
> Read 'em, John

Basers:

> Read 'em

Leader:

> Read 'em, John

Basers:

> Read 'em

Leader:

> Read 'em, ol' John

Basers:

> Read 'em

Leader:

> Read 'em, ol' John

Basers:

> Read 'em, oh, read 'em, let me go!

Leader:

> One by one, two by two, three by three and fo' by fo'
> Take all the members read 'em, oh
> Read 'em, let me go!
>
> Read 'em, John

(continue ad lib)

Read 'em, John

In This Field We Mus' Die

Sung by unidentified leader and group, Bolden, January 1, 1981.

Lawrence McKiver stated that the meaning of this song is "different ones know we going to die." He has a keener sense of metaphor than the author, who suggested that the "field" might refer to the fields in which the slaves toiled. "No, no, that mean *in this world*. The world is just like a field, you understand. You could go from here to any part of the world, you gon' be in it—and you die. That's the field of your trials and your life." This is one of the few shout songs in which the shouters of Bolden use harmony (in this instance, thirds) in the basers' refrain.

Leader:
> We mus' die

Basers:
> We mus'

Leader:
> Oh Lord,

Leader and basers:
> We mus' die.

Leader:
> In this fiel'

Basers:
> We mus'

Leader:
> Oh, Lord,

Leader and basers:
> We mus' die.

(similarly)
> We shall die /
> In that fiel' /
> We mus' die /
> In that fiel' /

(continue ad lib)

In This Field We Mus' Die

Alternate text, sung by Lawrence McKiver, July 29, 1994:

In this fiel'
   We mus'
Oh, Lord,
   We mus' die.
Everybody
   We mus'
Born to die
   We mus' die.
My God say
   We mus'
Sho's you live
   You gon' die.

(spoken)
All the medicine you can buy, all the doctors you can try, one of these days, you
gon' die.

Eve and Adam

Sung by Lawrence McKiver and group, Bolden, December 17, 1983
(Folkways Records FE 4344).

This shout has some of the most vivid pantomine, as the shouters
bend over to pick up imaginary leaves, suggesting Eve and Adam picking up
leaves to cover their nakedness. Parrish gives a version she "encountered in
Glynn and Camden Counties [which] holds to 'pinnin' leaves,'" and says "I
am inclined to believe that some McIntosh shouter took an artist's license
and substituted 'pickin' up' for 'pinnin' for the sake of more picturesque
action" (Parrish, p. 85). McKiver confirms this notion, emphasizing that
"pickin' up leaves" works better than "pinnin'," though pinnin' would be necessary to "make a garment." Robert W. Gordon collected the song and shout
as well and says: "In this song, the heavy sonorous call of God is answered by
the higher pitched, quicker reply of Eve, while at the proper places the
shouters stoop to the ground to pick up the leaves or go through the motions
of pinning them on" (Gordon, "The Negro Spiritual" in *Carolina Low Country*, pp. 201–202; see also McIlhenny, "Adam" in *Befo' the War Spirituals*,
p. 37, and "What a Trying Time" in *Slave Songs of the United States*, p. 74).
There are also secular frolic pieces related to this song, a typical one being North Carolina white musician J. E. Mainer's "Adam and Eve in the
Garden."

Leader:

>   Oh Eve, where is Adam?
>   Oh Eve, Adam in the garden
>   Pickin' up leaves.

>   God called Adam

Basers:

>   Pickin' up leaves

Leader:

>   God called Adam

Basers:

>   Pickin' up leaves.

Eve and Adam

(similarly)

God call y' Adam / Eve an' Adam /
My God call you / Why don't you answer? /
Why don' you answer? / Where is Adam? /
Eve an' Adam / Pickin', pickin' /
Pickin', pickin' / My God call you /
Why don' you answer? / Oh, Adam /
Oh, Adam / My God call you /
Pickin', pickin' / They was pickin' /
Eve an' Adam / My God call you /
My God call you / Why don' you answer? /
Hey, Adam! / Oh, Adam! /
My God call you / My God call you /
Why don' you answer? / Ol' Adam 'shamed /
Adam you 'shamed / My God call you /
He won' answer / Eve an' Adam /
Pickin', pickin' / Pickin', pickin' /
Eve an' Adam / They was a-pickin' /
My god call you / He won' answer /
Eve an' Adam / Adam is 'shamed /
Adam is 'shamed / Pickin', pickin' /
Eve an' Adam / Pickin', pickin' /

(continue ad lib)

Went to the Burial (Sinner Rock So)

Sung by Lawrence McKiver, Bolden, May 18, 1992.

This song presents a vivid picture of the entombment of Christ; the event is given immediacy by the use of the first person, "we went to the burial last night," and a shout is pictured around the sepulcher. When asked where he learned the song, McKiver replied: "My mother, that's some of my old ancestors' song. Oh, them folks, they could eat that song up, tear it up! They know how to blend in, blend in them words, just keep it goin' right on. It's beautiful. See, it has so many meanings to it." This song has one of the most beautiful melodies of the Bolden shout repertoire. The transcription here is from a solo performance by McKiver, in which he provides numerous variants on the leader's vocal line, as well as the refrain. The song is performed by the McIntosh County Shouters, whose basers use thirds in their singing—this harmonic treatment is notated below the transcription of McKiver's performance, as the shouters sang it at the Morton Theater, Athens, Georgia, June 25, 1994. William Francis Allen collected a variant, "Turn, Sinner, Turn O!" in Port Royal, South Carolina (*Slave Songs of the United States,* p. 36), which he called the "most dramatic of all the shouts."

Well we went to the burial las' night,
(spoken)
The background say
(sung)
We all buried Jesus
    Sinner rock so, sinner rock so.

Joseph prepared the body,
    Sinner rock so, sinner rock so.
Wrap him in a special cloth,
    Sinner wrap so, sinner weep so.

Mary weep and Martha moan,
    Sinner rock so, sinner rock so.

All night long,
    Sinner weep so, sinner rock so.
Weepin' and moanin'
    Sinner rock so, sinner rock so.

Mary weep and Martha moan,
    Sinner rock so, sinner rock so.
Jus' weepin' and moanin'!
    Sinner weep, sinner weep so.

Yes it was a sad time,
    Sinner weep so, Lord, sinner weep so.
They shout, shout, shout,
    Sinner weep, sinner weep so.
All around the sepulcher
    Sinner weep so, sinner weep so.

Yes, they crucified my Jesus!
    Sinner weep so, sinner weep so
Yes it was a sad time,
    Sinner rock so, sinner rock so.

Went to the Burial (Sinner Rock So)

9. They shout, shout,__ shout_____ *refrain* **C**

10. All a-round is a sep-ul-cher *refrain* **C**

11. Yes, they cru-ci-fied my Je-sus *refrain* **B**

12. Yes, they cru-ci-fied my Je-sus *refrain* **B**

13. Yes, it was a sad____ time____ *refrain* **B**

When the McIntosh County Shouters sing this song, they frequently add
the following harmony to the basers' refrain:

Sin-ner weep___ so,_____ Lord, sin-ner weep___ so_____

John on the Island, I Hear Him Groan

Sung by Lawrence McKiver and group, Bolden, September 5, 1981
(Folkways Records FE 4344).

McKiver's succession of vowel sounds—"Eli-ee-ay-Lord"—gives a richness to this chantlike song. Parrish gives a version titled "Eli Ah Can't Stan'," with the lines "hate that sin that made me moan" and "John's on the isle uh Pattemos" (Parrish, pp. 74–75). See also "John's on the Island on His Knees" (McIlhenny, *Befo' the War Spirituals,* pp. 154–55).

Leader:

John on the ilun, I hear him groan

Basers:

Eli, I can' stan'

Leader:

Eli-ee-ay-Lord

Basers:

Eli, I can' stan'

(similarly)
John went to heaven an' I'm so glad /
John on the ilun, I hear him groan /
Eli-ee-ay-Lord /
John on the ilun, I hear him groan /
John on the ilun, I hear him groan /
John on the ilun, I hear him groan /
Eli-ee-ay-Lord /
John went to heaven an' I'm so glad /
John went to heaven an' I'm so glad /
Eli-ee-ay-Lord /

(continue ad lib)

John on the Island, I Hear Him Groan

Walk through the Valley in the Field

Walk through the Valley in the Field

Sung by group, Bolden, January 1, 1982.

This hymn-like song is one of the few nonantiphonal shout songs; it is a favorite for the Watch Night shout and is sung by the McIntosh County Shouters at their public performances as a kind of shout processional as they enter the stage. William Francis Allen recovered a variant, "We Will March through the Valley" in Virginia (*Slave Songs of the United States*, p. 73).

Walk through the valley in the field
Walk through the valley in the field,
My Lord call me and I mus' go,
Walk through the valley in the field.
    Oh members
(Repeat verse)
    Oh sinner
(Repeat verse)

Ezekiel Saw That Little Stone

Sung by Lawrence McKiver and group, Bolden, September 5, 1981.

Lawrence McKiver suggested in a conversation on July 29, 1994, that the prophet referred to in this shout song should be Isaiah rather than Ezekiel. "Them old folks had them songs, they'd read them songs from the Bible, they didn't have quite the learnin', but they had good understanding. . . . They would catch it from the Bible; all different prophets had a vision of the comin' of Jesus Christ. . . . You say I dream about a man, I dream about him in a different view, and that's the way they raised the song. Like, Ezekiel saw him as a wheel in the middle of a wheel, Isaiah saw him as a stone, rollin' out the mountain, not by han'." Lawrence learned this song from his Uncle Henry, the husband of his Aunt Sarah. James Weldon Johnson gives a closely related variant of this song, "Daniel Saw De Stone" (*The Second Book of Negro Spirituals*, 1926, p. 162).

Leader:

Ezekiel saw that little stone

Basers:

Rollin', rollin'

Leader:

Ezekiel saw that little stone

Rollin' up the mountain not by han'

(similarly)

John saw that little stone /

Who you reckon is that little stone? /

King Jesus is that little stone /

John saw that little stone /

Ezekiel saw that little stone /

Ezekiel Saw That Little Stone

Lay Down, Body

Sung by Lawrence McKiver with group, St. Simons Island, August 20, 1983 (Folkways Records FE 4344).

The apocalyptic imagery of this song, combined with Lawrence McKiver's emotional and masterful performance, makes this a high point of African American traditional singing. The energetic interplay of leader and chorus is especially strong here, with an effect that McKiver calls "choppin'." In Johann Buis's analysis, the singer's "short motive allows for flamboyant improvisation within a very constricted time span." The singer and basers here confront contrasting images of the protagonist's physical body both yearning for rest after a life of travail and bursting from the tomb. The lines "You been toilin'" and the idea of the singer resting a little while occur in the spiritual "Sit Down, Servant," as God greeting his servant who has "come over." The set of words sung here are older verses, but recently McKiver has added to the song. He explained, "I put a lot of words to 'Lay Down, Body.' If you ever pay attention, they [the basers] be shootin' me, [they] would say 'Lay down a little while,' that's the background. I say: 'I know you're tired . . . you been toilin' / in the rain and cold / I know you're tired / so lay down, body/ and take yo' res' / you don't worry / my God'll wake you / and when he call / tombstone movin'/ grave is a-bustin'/ you'll be happy / join hands with the angels/ you sing and shout / all around God's throne / sing glory hallelu- jah / I'm so glad / my trouble is over / I made it home / I made it home at las'.' You ever see how they be poundin' me with the body, but every time they pound me, I got somethin' new to tell 'em about it, see?" He said the old people sang about the "tombstone movin'" and "grave is a-bustin'," but the last scene of the person joining hands with the angels and singing and shouting around God's throne is his own (interview, February 12, 1994). For a South Carolina performance, see "Lay Down, Body," sung by Bertha Smith and the Moving Star Hall Singers, recorded on Johns Island by Guy Carawan (*Been in the Storm So Long;* Folkways Records 3842). Another Johns Island variant was recorded in 1987 by Thomas Earl Hawley, Jr. (*The Slave Tradition of Singing Among the Gullah of Johns Island,* South Caro- lina, pp. 54–56).

Leader:

Lay down, body

Basers:

Lay down a little while

Leader:

Lay down, body

Basers:

Lay down a little while

I know you're tired / Lay down, body /
I know you're tired / Lay down, body /
You is tired / Soul need restin' /
Don't you worry / He gonna call you /
When He call / Tombstone movin' /
Grave is bustin' / Soul is risin' /
Oh, body! / This ol' body /
I know you tired / Soul need restin' /
You been toilin' / Long time /
Yo' soul need restin' / You don' worry /
My God call you / And when He call /
He will wake you / Tombstone movin'! /
Grave is a-bustin' /soul is a-risin'! /
Oh, body! / Lay down, body /
I know you tired / Soul need restin' /
Oh, body / This ol' body /
Lay down, body / Lay down, body /
Soul an' body / Need some restin' /
Oh, body / This ol' body /
My God call you / And when he call /
He will wake you / Tombstone movin' /
Grave is a-bustin' / Soul be risin' /
Oh, body! / This ol' body /
Need some restin' / Need some restin' /
You been toilin' / A long time /
I know you tired / I know you tired /
Oh, body / This ol' body /
Soon one mornin' / Grave is bustin' /
Tombstone movin' / Oh, body! /
Oh, body / Lay down, body /
Lay down, body / Oh, body /

Soul and body / I know you tired /
You been toilin' / A long time /
I know you tired / Lay down, body /
Lay down, body / Oh, body /
My God wake you / An' tombstone— /
Grave is a-bustin' / Soul is a-risin' /
Oh, body / Soul an' body /
I know you tired / soul needs restin' /
Oh, body

Lay Down, Body

Watch That Star

Sung by Lawrence McKiver with group, Bolden, December 17, 1983 (Folkways Records FE 4434).

According to McKiver, the chorus of this song is an old shout song, and the verse is his addition. "When I sing the song, I get a touching word from the hymn. I put that to the song: 'Well the days is past and gone / The evening shadows 'pear. / Oh may we all remember well / That the night of death draws near.' You see, understand? You see, as a person watching me, it comes from the gospel hymn book, I put that in. The days is always passing and going, the evening shadow of death is always near to you, understand?" In answer to our question of what the old people sang, he replied, "They would sing 'Watch that star, see how it run.' They didn't put in the touching words like I put in. It would worry me to sing it the way they sing it. I move out from it so far, to bracket them. They didn't sing it the way I do" (interview, February 12, 1994). While he usually adheres fairly closely to traditional texts, in such instances as this, McKiver feels he must rework or add to a song to keep it viable for him in practice. The hymn he used is "Evening Shade," written by John Leland in 1835; McKiver's adaptation is more vernacular than the original, with "death will soon disrobe us all of what we here possess" becoming "rob us all." In the shout for this song, the participants extend their arms to the heavens in an eloquent gesture. Johann Buis comments: "Rather than the call-and-response patterns common in . . . ring shout songs, this song consists of an extended melody sung by the leader and then repeated by the group. The slightly syncopated elements counterbalance the melodious (*cantilena*) nature of the song. The profoundly theological statement of Christ suffering and the singer going free is a rhetorical point which arrives at the melodic climax, heightening the musical and linguistic effect."

Chorus (sung solo):

> Oh, watch that star, see how it run
> Watch that star, see how it run,
> If the star run down in the western hills,
> You oughtta watch that star, see how it run,

Leader:

      Everybody—

Chorus (leader and basers):

      Oh, watch that star, see how it run

      Watch that star, see how it run,

      If the star run down in the western hills,

      You oughtta watch that star, see how it run,

      Oh, members—

Chorus (leader and basers):

      Oh, watch that star, see how it run

      Watch that star, see how it run,

      If the star run down in the western hills,

      You oughtta watch that star, see how it run,

Leader:

      Well the days is past and gone

      The evenin' shadow 'pear,

      Oh may we all remember well

      The night of death drawin' near

         Everybody—

Chorus (leader and basers):

      Oh, watch that star, see how it run

      Watch that star, see how it run,

      If the star run down in the western hills,

      You oughtta watch that star, see how it run,

Leader:

      Oh, members—

Chorus (leader and basers):

      Oh, watch that star, see how it run

      Watch that star, see how it run,

      If the star run down in the western hills,

      You oughtta watch that star, see how it run,

Leader:

      Well we lay our garment by,

      Upon our bed to res';

      Oh death will soon rob us all

      Of what we have possess'

         Everybody—

Chorus (as above, and repeat previous verse and chorus)

Watch That Star

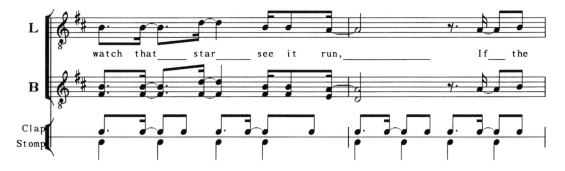

watch that___ star___ see it run,_____ If__ the

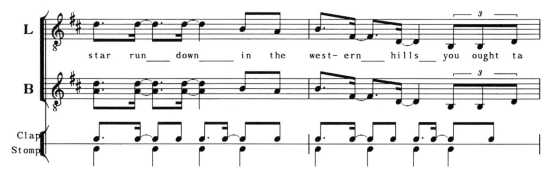

star run___ down_____ in the west- ern___ hills___ you ought ta

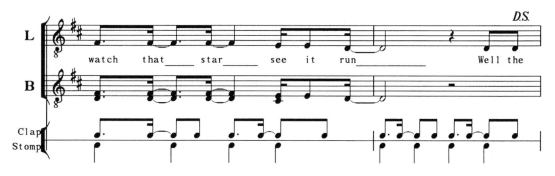

watch that____ star_____ see it run_____ Well the

Farewell, Last Day Goin'

Sung by Lawrence McKiver and group, Bolden, December 17, 1983 (Folkways Records FE 4434).

In some communities "Yonder Come Day" was sung traditionally at the dawn of a New Year after Watch Night; in Bolden, a variant, "Happy Angel, Day's A-Comin'" was used; nowadays "Farewell, Last Day Goin'" is sung at the close of the Watch Night Shout and is used to conclude public performances of the shout as well. The basers sing the refrain as "farewell las' goin'," but when McKiver demonstrates the way he believes the refrain properly should be sung, he sings it "farewell, las' day goin'," adding rhythmic interest to the line. Singers and shouters wave goodbye during the performance of this shout. Lydia Parrish gives a related song from St. Simons Island, "Good-bye, Everybody" (Parrish, pp. 91–92).

Leader:

    This is the las'

Basers:

    Farewell, las' goin', farewell

Leader:

    This is the las'

Basers:

    Farewell, las' goin', farewell

Leader:

Goodbye, members / Goodbye, members / I hate to leave you / I hope to see you / Goodbye, members / Goodbye, members / This is the las'/ This is the las' / We had a good time / I hate to leave you / I hope to see you / Another time / This is the las' / Goodbye, members / Goodbye, members / I hate to leave you / I hope to see you / Oh, this is the las' / Oh, this is the las' / This is the las' / Goodbye, members / Ah, members / Bye-bye, members / I hate to leave you / We had a good time / I hate to leave you / I hope to see you / Oh, this is the las' / This is the las' / This is the las' / Oh, this is the las' / This is the las' / Goodbye, members!

Farewell, Last Day Goin'

Transcriber's Note

Johann S. Buis

Upon first hearing the ring shout repertory, even the sophisticated listener can be fooled by the simplicity of the musical construction. But this simplicity is deceptively complex. The improvisational artistry of the leader's singing is so fleeting and varied that putting such virtuosity on paper has been an extremely daunting task. Indeed, the agogic glides, falsetto swoops, and highly syncopated gestures that the leader generates in such songs as "Eve and Adam," "John on the Island," "Went to the Burial," and numerous others have not been rendered in minute detail in these transcriptions. Such complex gestures are virtually impossible to notate. A middle ground of readable renderings that are neither overly simplistic nor unduly complex has been the guiding concept for the transcriptions. The virtuosity of the leader is often juxtaposed by the simplicity of the basers' response (see "Eve and Adam"). The transcriptions bear out this phenomenon.

Throughout, the transcriptions are rendered with the upper staff for the leader, the lower staff for the basers, and the rhythm notated below these staffs. Rarely, in cases of unison singing (e.g., "Watch That Star") or solo singing (e.g., "Drive Ol' Joe") has a single staff been used. The rhythmic patterns have been notated as "clap" and "stomp" on separate lines. Occasionally, an additional line has been added (designated "feet"). Participants generally clap a pattern, the "sticker(s)" stomp another pattern (often identical), and the same "stickers" tap their feet (alternately) coinciding with the use of the stick. On other occasions the heels might simply tap four quarter notes in a measure on the beat throughout; in such a case the third line has been used.

The rhythmic patterns, though generally the characteristic syncopated pattern underlying the entire repertoire of ring shout songs, vary subtly from song to song. In some, the "clap" pattern and the "stomp" pattern coincide exactly with one another, as described above. In other cases, a polyrhythmic pattern results when participants overlay varying rhythmic patterns with one another. Here, too, the transcriptions reflect a rendering that does not record the minutest detail of the polyrhythmic pattern, but rather the perceptible patterns that can be notated accurately and recreated by the reader.

During the slow introduction of many songs (what the shouters call "setting" the song), there is never any rhythmic accompaniment, but the leading baser coerces the group to join him as soon as the lively tempo begins following the "setting." Rarely does this "coercion" start on the downbeat (beginning) of a measure. Usually, the leading baser leads up to the beginning of the cycle with everyone in place. This process usually occurs within a split second. No attempt has been made to notate this "coercive" practice. Instead, all parts of the basers' pattern have been rendered simultaneously in the transcriptions.

Melodic characteristics have been quite complex. Transcription has been affected by the following factors:

1. Shifting centonization. A phenomenon that shifts the point of gravity incrementally higher or lower. This practice causes the transcriber to lose a point of reference. In such cases, the beginning point of reference has remained fixed in the transcription. Despite the shifting centonation, internal intervallic relationships remain exceptionally accurate, beyond the "setting" phase.

2. Absence of versification. No verses exist in any songs. Rather, the call-and-response structure makes responses fairly easy and predictable. Interestingly, the more ornate segments ("calls" in the call-and-response structure) appear much later in recordings used for this project. In the interest of practicality, the variants have been listed

with text below them. These variants are not always complete, but in the nature of fluid improvisatory practice, they are no doubt representative of the leader's art.

3. Identical texts do not have identical melodies. As in "Eve and Adam" the same words carry different melodies, particularly in the leader's calls.

4. The rapid melodic cells that constitute many of the leader's calls frequently take .75 seconds, compounding the transcriber's task enormously.

5. Overlapping entries. Occasionally, the leader and basers overlap their entries (see "Army Cross Over"), presenting the transcriber with a challenge that seems fairly easy on paper and that lends an attractive flow to the singing.

6. Keys of convenience. A number of songs have been transposed within one half-step up or down, making the key signatures no more than three sharps or flats (one song was sung in F-sharp major, another in B major; six and five sharps respectively). This choice was made for two reasons: first, the convenience of reading, and second, the fact that the same song can be sung in one key on one occasion and another neighboring key on another occasion. Such pitch centonation fluctuates between a half-step to a minor third apart.

The challenges presented here are rendered with the intention that they should be easily reconstructed for persons wanting to acquaint themselves with the artistic practices. As with any project of this nature, the excellence of the performances will be best understood by listening to recordings. Dr. Kevin Kelly and Mr. David Enete have graciously assisted in the preparation of the manuscript and the rhythmic examples, respectively. I owe them a great debt.

Historical Essay

The Ring Shout

Revisiting the Islamic and African Issues of a Christian "Holy Dance"

Johann S. Buis

Lorenzo Dow Turner's explanation that the word "shout" comes from the Arabic word *saut* (Parrish 1942; 1965) is one theory of the likely origin of the term. There can be no doubt that the performance context of the ring shout never involves any shouting in the literal sense of the word.[1] Such empirical practice would give credence to an argument that underscores the absence of shouting in the ring shout. However there is another theory which holds that the etymological origin of the ring shout goes back to Norse (especially Scandinavian languages), Middle Dutch, and Middle English, which does confirm the vocal shouting present in the term.[2] It is understandable that American English usage could have transferred the term to the African American context. The question is: did the term originate with either theory, or other theories, or is the understanding of the term a conflation of the two theories? Though this question cannot be answered for certain, the Arabic context of the term adds an intriguing dimension to the debate. One would have to suspend this discussion for a moment. First, one has to place the debate squarely within the context of its African origin.

Counterclockwise dance forms have survived throughout sub-Saharan Africa—the ancestral home of black American slaves—for centuries in primarily ritualistic contexts. Writers, such as Gordon, who argued that the shout was a "double quick, tripping measure . . . ," Krehbiel, who pointed to the march variant of the shout, and Courlander, who regarded the shout as dancing, confirm that the circular nature of the dance is deeply embedded in the symbolic implications of its African origin.[3] Therefore the symbolic presence of strong African ritual confirms the undeniable African origin of the ring shout.

The second issue that one must consider (before examining the Arabic issue and the ring shout) is the African nature of the rhythmic signature. Rhythmic signatures as a characteristic of analysis regrettably are undervalued in Western analytical tools. McClary and Walser have lamented the fact that Europe-derived analysis favors abstract patterns of pitch and form at the expense of rhythm criteria.[4] The pattern that basers and the chorus clap consistently in all ring shout compositions is commonly referred to as the 3+3+2 pattern. In a recent seminal article on rhythm analysis, Jay Rahn has argued convincingly for the ubiquitous nature of this syncopated pattern in African-derived music. Surveying the literature from Nicholas Ballanta-Taylor (1922), Don Knowlton (1926), Aaron Copland (1927), Winthrop Sargeant (1938), Ernest Bornemann (1946), and Marshall Stearns (1956) to Gunther Schuller (1968), the presence of the 3+3+2 pattern is established in African patterns, jazz, and similar contexts.[5] Rahn provides the basic pattern and some variants in this form:

Basic 3+3+2 rhythm

♩.   ♩.   ♩

Close variants

All kinds of variants appear in "a walking bass line in swing and later styles, a stride bass in piano rags and other march-related forms, or steady strumming in quarters by banjo or guitar in New Orleans, Chicago, and other early jazz idioms."[6] This point illustrates the centrality of the ring shout rhythm in a variety of derivative African American music forms. Having established the African symbolism of the ring shout and its rhythmic content, the Arabic facet requires further examination.

In his seminal book, *African Muslims in Antebellum America: A Sourcebook*, Allan D. Austin gives convincing evidence that the Muslim presence among African slaves was particularly evident on the Eastern Seaboard, including Georgia.[7] Not only was the Muslim presence evident among new slaves—however secretive the practices might have been—but during the period 1730–1860 proof of the Islamic presence is documented in Austin's sourcebook. However small their number, the fact that Islamic converts had lived in the ancestral West African regions before the slave trade to the Americas lends some credence to the influence, not origin, of the *saut* (Arabic-Islamic) theory behind the ring shout. During 1995 a new dissertation on Muslim American slaves and their narratives appeared, exploring religion and cultural accommodation among this lesser-known group of slaves.[8] Were one to assume that elements of Muslim musical practice entered the highly syncretistic nature of counterclockwise religious ritual dances of slaves, and that remnants of such a practice are still evident in the coastal regions where the ring shout survived, examining the influence of Islamic practices might be a logical step to take.

Although the syncretistic practices mask many disparate influences, it is possible to consider an Islamic influence upon the ring shout without claiming that this influence is the source or origin of the entire genre. The preponderance of the evidence favoring the indigenous African animistic origin of the genre would negate the claim of an Islamic origin for the ring shout. Nonetheless it is instructive that we examine the parallels of the ring shout in Islamic practice. Even a small ingredient would flavor the ancient African ring shout soup. Therefore the rest of this essay concentrates on the possible Islamic influences, not origins, which surface in the ring shout. First one needs to divert to examine the etymological dimension of *saut*. Thereafter Islamic practice and rhythmic practice will give further insight into the topic.

Upon closer examination, the term *saut* presents problematic etymological description. The common use of this term today simply is to mean "sound." During the seventh century—the period of the orthodox *khalifs*

(A.D. 632–662)—the term specifically meant "verses that were set to music," according to the *Kitab al-aghani* (Farmer 1929; 1967). Later in his text Farmer presents further evidence of the vocal prominence in the concept *saut,* rendering the translation of Galen's Latin treatise *De voce* into Arabic as *Kitab al-saut.* Hunain ibn Ishaq al-'Ibadi, Abu Zaid (809–873) wrote the ninth-century Latin-Arabic translation of Galen's *De voce.*

Despite the original emphasis on poetic song and the voice as central to the concept of *saut,* the use of the term meaning "sound" was current at the time Hunain translated Galen's treatise. A contemporary of Hunain's, the theorist Al-Kindi (d. 874), discussed Greek music theory, using such terms as *saut* for sound, *ab'ad* for intervals, *ajnas* for genres, and so on (Farmer 1929; 1967). It is in this latter sense that the concept of *saut* has remained the word for "sound" today, despite the association of singing and rhythmic beating (sound?) with *saut* as the two indispensable elements for understanding the ring shout.

The element of ecstasy present in earlier ring shout performances occasioned participants falling out because they were moved by the "sperrit."[9] Though entrance into a near-trance state is common in ritual practice of Africa, the presence of this practice in Islamic Africa is rarely brought into context of the ring shout. Twining confirms this parallel connection, saying that the Sea Islanders "rely on vibrational patterns to change their consciousness" in a similar manner as "the healing sodalities of ululating women in [Islamic] North Africa."[10] Therefore, as one argues for the added layer of an Islamic presence upon the indigenous sub-Saharan African origin of the shout in Africa, the possession factor discussed here presents yet another gateway to enter the Islamic-influence-on-the-shout debate.

The persistent use of the same rhythmic pattern in all the songs of the ring shout genre leads us to further investigation. This rhythmic pattern, it has been argued above, is undeniably ubiquitous in African and African-derived musical forms. While the use of polyrhythmic elements of certain songs ("Kneebone Bend," for instance) is certainly characteristic of African rhythmic usage, the ever-present single rhythmic pattern accompanying each song hints at a prominent characteristic of Islamic-Arabic dance music practice. Indeed, this issue became apparent to the McIntosh County Shouters at a performance on August 6, 1994, at the Atlanta Black Arts Festival. An Egyptian troupe had performed on that occasion and displayed the prominence of single rhythmic patterns, which intrigued the shouters. Such information is good circumstantial evidence at best.

However a book published in 1976 presents the most compelling evidence that parallels the Arabic *saut* with the rhythmic practice of the ring shout. Before investigating that source, a comment about the melodic use of ring shout songs is timely. Melodically this musical genre shows no resemblance to any Arabic melodic structures based upon scalar formulas called *maqamat.* Indeed the melodic characteristics of ring shout songs show indigenous African melodic characteristics (e.g., call-and-response, mimetic devices, heterophony, etc.), common in all early African American sacred and secular repertory. Additional characteristics include opening triadic centonation (almost always a minor triad), minute glissandi around stable gravitational pitches, cadential and motivic elements, and the like. It is the melodic signature common to many African-derived songs in the United States that have accounted for overlooking the Arabic influence upon the ring shout genre. Now to return to the rhythmic signature that points to the Arabic element in the ring shout's evolution.

Jean Jenkins and Poul Olsen, in their book *Music and Musical Instruments in the World of Islam,* write that the term *saut* in Bahrain designates a particular song genre. Here the importance of the term designating a song genre is noteworthy as the term should denote "sound" in common Arabic parlance. Such a genre designation of the *saut* parallels the *genre* designation of the ring shout. Therefore it would seem logical to examine the principal rhythmic accompaniment of the Bahrainian *saut* (as the only existing *saut* genre today) with the rhythmic pattern central to the ring shout. The characteristic rhythmic accompaniment to the Bahrainian *saut* is remarkably similar to that of the ring shout. Two variants of the *saut* pattern from Bahrain are:

Compare the two variants of that pattern with the ring shout pattern:

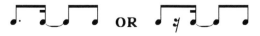

and a proportional variant:

$$ \mathmove{} \quad \text{♩.} \qquad \text{♩.} \qquad \text{♩} $$

Although both the Bahrainian *saut* and the McIntosh County ring shout patterns are not identical, the similarity is close enough for them to be related. Both share similar characteristics: the same striking downbeat, the syncopated second sound with a rapid upbeat return to the downbeat. Taking into account the possible modification that rhythmic patterns undergo as they transmigrate to different cultural environs, the identity of the two rhythmic patterns is close enough for a significant resemblance.

It is worth noting that Bahrain and the Georgia Sea Island coast are significantly remote enough that it is likely that this rhythmic agreement could attest to the longevity of the *saut* and ring shout as retained within remote, isolated localities, paralleled by their mutual rhythmic similarities. Might it be that as the McIntosh County Shouters are the last remaining representatives of the ring shout genre, the Bahrainian *saut* might be in danger of dying out? That question is for another investigation. So, too, is a discussion of the rhythmic signature of the African-European-derived fife-and-drum repertoire of the Mississippi Delta. In that case, the drum cadence used for all fife melodies has a remarkable resemblance to the ring shout rhythm of the McIntosh County Shouters (cf. Buis 1994). For now this essay ends with its initial premise of exploring Islamic and indigenous African issues surrounding the ring shout, a sacred Christian dance.

Notes

Introduction. "We Never Let It Go By"

1. Interview, August 7, 1981.

2. Turner, Lorenzo Dow, *Africanisms in the Gullah Dialect* (1949; reprint, Ann Arbor: University of Michigan Press, 1949). Turner defines the Arabic *saut* as "a religious ring dance in which the participants continue to perform until exhausted" and cites an Arabic verb, *sauwata,* meaning to run until exhausted (p. 202). Accounts of the North American coastal ring shout frequently describe the participants continuing until they tire.

3. Notes to *On One Accord: Singing and Praying Bands of Tidewater Maryland and Delaware,* Global Village CD 225; produced by Jonathan David and Michael Schlesinger, annotated by Jonathan David.

4. Interview, August 7, 1981.

5. Bessie Jones and Bess Lomax Hawes, *Step It Down: Games, Plays, Songs, and Stories from the Afro-American Heritage* (1972; reprint, Athens: University of Georgia Press, 1987), p. 143.

6. Another remarkable African survival has recently surfaced in McIntosh County. Mary Moran, a seventy-five-year-old resident of the Harris Neck Community, a few miles north of Bolden, has remembered a funeral song in the Mende language of Sierra Leone that she learned from her late mother, Ameilia Dawley. Prompted by ethnomusicologist Cynthia Schmidt's playing of a recording of Dawley made in the 1930s by Lorenzo Dow Turner, Ms. Moran was able to sing the song, which had been passed down by women through the generations since the forced voyage from Africa. Unlike the Bolden ring shout tradition, which was unbroken in community practice, Moran's rare African song was held in inactive memory until recently. She has continued the chain of tradition by teaching it to her granddaughter; she also sings it in public performance, on at least one occasion during a program with the McIntosh County Shouters. Jingle Davis, "Survival of the Gullah," *Atlanta Journal-Constitution,* November 7, 1996, G-1.

1. "Kneebone in the Wilderness"

From *The Griots,* Folkways FE 4178, recorded by Samuel Charters. This powerful song presents a unique description of the slave trade from an African perspective. The song is sung in Mandingo, but the terms "slave house" and "American Negroes" are sung in English.

1. Spoken introduction to "Kneebone Bend" by Lawrence McKiver, December 13, 1983.

2. Robert Farris Thompson, *African Art in Motion* (Los Angeles: University of California Press, 1974), 80–82.

3. Betty J. Crouther, "Iconography of a Henry Gudgell Walking Stick," *Southeastern College Art Conference Review* vol. 12, no. 3, 1993; cites Patrick R. McNaughton, "Bamana Blacksmiths," *African Arts* 12 (February 1979).

4. Thompson, *African Art,* 32. Thompson cites I. Schapera, *The Early Cape Hottentots* (Capetown, S. Afr.: Van Riebeek Society, n.d.), 139.

5. Ibid., 32. Lorna Marshall, "Kung Bushmen Religious Beliefs," *Africa* 2 (1962), 249.

6. James W. Covington, *The Seminoles of Florida* (Gainesville: University Press of Florida, 1993), 94.

7. Louis Capron, "The Medicine Bundles of the Florida Seminole and the Green Corn Dance," in *Anthropological Papers* 35, Smithsonian Institution Bulletin no. 151, reprinted in William Sturdevant, ed., *A Seminole Source Book* (New York: Garland Publishing, 1987), 197.

8. Frank G. Speck, "Ethnology of the Yuchi Indians" in *Anthropological Publications, University of Pennsylvania,* vol. 1 (Philadelphia: University Museum, 1909), 124.

9. Elaine Nichols, ed., *The Last Miles of the Way: African-American Homegoing Traditions, 1890–Present* (Columbia: South Carolina State Museum, 1989). Nichols cites Stuckey's *Slave Culture,* 12, and Robert Farris Thompson's *Flash of the Spirit: African and Afro-American Art* (New York: Random House, 1983), 109–110.

10. Thompson, *Flash of the Spirit,* 108.

11. Ibid, 111.

12. Georgia Writers' Project (Savannah Unit), Works Projects Administration, *Drums and Shadows: Survival Studies Among the Georgia Coastal Negroes* (1940; Athens: University of Georgia Press, 1986), 180.

13. Harold Courlander, *Negro Folk Music, U.S.A.* (New York: Columbia University Press, 1963), 200.

14. Letitia Burwell, *Plantation Reminiscences,* 57, quoted in Dena J. Epstein,

Sinful Tunes and Spirituals: Black Folk Music to the Civil War (Urbana: University of Illinois Press, 1977), 130.

15. Stuckey, *Slave Culture,* 87.

16. Albert J. Raboteau, *Slave Religion: The "Invisible Institution" in the Antebellum South* (Oxford: Oxford University Press, 1978), 72–73.

17. William Francis Allen, Charles Pickard Ware, Lucy McKim Garrison, *Slave Songs of the United States,* with a new introduction by W. K. McNeil (1867; reprint, Baltimore: Clearfield Co., 1992), xii–xiii.

18. Erskine Clarke, *Wrestlin' Jacob* (Atlanta: John Knox Press, 1979), 46–47.

19. Charles Colcock Jones, *Suggestions,* 39–40, quoted in Epstein, 201.

20. Epstein, 192–94.

21. Charles Ball, *Slavery in the United States: A Narrative of the Life and Adventures of Charles Ball, a Black Man, Who Lived Forty Years in Maryland, South Carolina and Georgia as a Slave* . . . (New York: J. S. Taylor, 1837), 164–65, 201–203, quoted in Epstein, 193.

22. Courlander, *Negro Folk Music,* 195.

23. Epstein, 124, quotes Henry W. Ravenel, "Recollections of Southern Plantation Life," *Yale Review* 25 (June 1936), 768–69.

24. Freddie Palmer told of "Walk, Billy Arbor," a ring play, being performed "with the rest of the [shouts]" on Christmas night and New Year's Eve. Interview, February 12, 1994.

25. Sir Charles Lyell, *A Second Visit to the United States of North America* (New York: Harper & Brothers, 1849), quoted in Epstein, 233.

26. Epstein, 233.

27. Ibid., 233.

28. Ibid., 233; Epstein quotes Parsons, *Inside View of Slavery* (Boston: J. P. Jewett, 1855), 276.

29. "An Englishman in South Carolina, December 1860 and July 1862, Part 2," *Continental Monthly* 3 (Jan. 1863), 110–17, quoted in Epstein, 234.

30. Georgia Bryan Conrad, *Reminiscences of a Southern Woman* (Hampton, Va.: Hampton Institute Press, [n.d.]), 9.

31. Roger D. Abrahams, *Singing the Master: The Emergence of African American Culture in the Plantation South* (New York: Pantheon Books, 1992), xxiv.

32. Stuckey, *Slave Culture,* 89–90.

33. Courlander, *Slave Culture,* 197. This shout song, alternately titled "Run Old Jeremiah" and "Run, Jeremiah" (recorded in June 1934 by John A. Lomax and Alan Lomax in Jennings, Louisiana, for the Archives of American Folk Song in the Library of Congress), was sung by Joe Washington and Coleman Austin, who were described in the information accompanying entry AFS 108A2 as "two Negro boys."

In his annotation to the release of this performance, currently available as Library of Congress cassette AFS L2, Alan Lomax explained that "the community had recently reintroduced the ring-shout as a means of attracting and holding in the church the young people who wanted to dance."

34. Guion Griffis Johnson, *A Social History of the Sea Islands* (Chapel Hill: University of North Carolina Press, 1930), 36.

35. Ibid., 154–55.

36. Epstein's reference to Higginson, 280; her chapter on the editors of *Slave Songs of the United States*, 303–20.

37. Epstein, 278.

38. Ibid., 281; Epstein quotes Higginson's *Diary* manuscript, Houghton Library, Harvard University, and notes that Higginson's published versions "lack the immediacy of the original diary entry."

39. William Francis Allen, *Diary, 1863–1866 II* (manuscript). State Historical Society of Wisconsin, entry for December 25, 1863, published in Epstein, 284–85.

40. Stuckey, *Slave Culture*, 85.

41. Originally published in the *Continental Monthly* (August 1863); quoted in Bernard Katz, ed., *The Social Implications of Early Negro Music in the United States* (New York: Arno Press, 1969), 4–5.

42. Marcel [W. F. Allen], *Nation* I (New York, December 14, 1865), 744–45. Reprinted in Bruce Jackson, *The Negro and his Folklore in Nineteenth-Century Periodicals* (Austin: University of Texas Press, 1967), 79.

43. Ibid., 79.

44. W. K. McNeil's introduction to the 1992 edition of *Slave Songs of the United States*, 5.

45. *Slave Songs*, iv–v.

46. *New York Nation*, May 30, 1867; in *Slave Songs*, xiii–xiv.

47. *Slave Songs*, xiv–xv.

48. Interview with Lawrence McKiver, October 18, 1983.

49. Thompson, *African Art*, 43–44. The last reference is to Gerald D. Suttles, "The Social Order of the Slums" in *Ethnicity and Territory in the Inner City* (Chicago: University of Chicago Press, 1968), 62–66.

50. *Slave Songs*, xv.

51. M. R. S., "Visitor's Account," 6, an account of an after school shout by children in Beaufort, South Carolina, in 1866; published in Epstein, 281.

52. Towne, letters and diary, 20. Letter, "St. Helena's, Sunday, April 27, 1862." Quoted in Epstein, 282.

53. Rubin Tomlinson to James Miller McKim, October 5, 1862, MS Cornell University Library. Quoted in Epstein, 284.

54. Pearson, *Letters from Port Royal*, 292–93. Quoted in Epstein, 286.

55. Charlotte Forten, *Life on the Sea Islands*, 1864, 594.

56. Charles W. Joyner, *Folk Song in South Carolina* (Columbia: University of South Carolina Press, 1971), 72.

57. *Slave Songs*, xix.

58. *National Anti-Slavery Standard* 22 (October 12, 1861), [3]; quoted in Epstein, 244.

59. *Slave Songs*, xvii–xviii.

60. *Drums and Shadows*, 149–50.

61. Ibid., 159.

62. Jones and Hawes, *Step It Down*, 143.

63. Parrish, *Slave Songs*, 85.

64. Henry Edward Krehbiel, *Afro-American Folksongs: A Study in Racial and National Music* (New York: G. Schirmer, 1914), 33.

65. William Wells Brown, *My Southern Home* (1880; reprint, Upper Saddle River, N.J.: Gregg Press, 1968), 191; quoted in Stuckey, *Slave Culture*, 63.

66. Stuckey, op. cit., 85.

67. Jonathan David, notes to *On One Accord: Singing and Praying Bands of Tidewater Maryland and Delaware*, Global Village CD 225, 1992, 10.

68. Ibid., 11.

69. Bishop Daniel Alexander Payne, *Recollections of Seventy Years* (Nashville: Publishing House of the A.M.E. Sunday School Union, 1883; reprint, Arno Press and the *New York Times*, 1968).

70. Ibid., 255.

71. David, *On One Accord*, 11.

72. Ibid., 12.

73. James Weldon Johnson, *The Book of American Negro Spirituals* (New York: Viking Press, 1925), 32–33.

74. Robert W. Gordon, "The Negro Spiritual," in Augustine T. Smythe, Herbert Ravenel Sass, et al., *The Carolina Low Country* (New York: Macmillan, 1931), 198–201.

75. Ibid., 201.

76. Ibid.

77. Abrahams, *Singing the Master*, 141.

78. Rudi Blesh and Harriet Janis, *They All Played Ragtime* (New York: Alfred A. Knopf, 1950; rev. ed., New York: Oak Publications, 1966), 188–89.

79. Ibid., 190.

80. Scott E. Brown, *James P. Johnson: A Case of Mistaken Identity* (Metuchen, N.J.: Scarecrow Press and the Institute of Jazz Studies, Rutgers University, 1982), 22.

81. Ibid., 171–72.

82. Zora Neale Hurston, *The Sanctified Church* (Berkeley: Turtle Island, 1981), 103, quoted in Stuckey, *Slave Culture,* 97.

83. James Baldwin, *Go Tell It on the Mountain* (New York: Dell, 1952), 14, quoted in Stuckey, *Slave Culture,* 97.

84. P. Smiley, "Folk-Lore from Va., S.C., Ga., Ala., and Fla.," *Journal of American Folklore* 32 (1919), 378. Quoted in Newbell Niles Puckett, *Folk Beliefs of the Southern Negro* (Chapel Hill: University of North Carolina Press, 1926), 59.

85. Phillips Barry, "Negro Folk-Songs from Maine," in *Bulletin of the Folk-Song Society of the Northeast* 8, Cambridge, Mass.: Powell Printing Company, 1934. Reprint, Philadelphia: American Folklore Society, 1960, 14.

86. Barry, "Negro Folk-Songs from Maine: The Shout," *Bulletin* 9, 10.

87. Ibid.

88. Turner, *Africanisms,* 202.

89. Barry, "Negro Folk-Songs," 12.

90. Ibid., 11–12.

91. Krehbiel, *Afro-American Folksongs,* 63.

92. Barry, op. cit., 12.

93. T. J. Woofter, Jr., *Black Yeomanry: Life on St. Helena Island* (1930; reprint, New York: Octagon Books, 1978), 219–20, 233.

94. Guy Carawan's description of watch on Johns Island, 1959; quoted in Joyner, *Folk Song in South Carolina,* 73.

95. Guy Carawan with Candie Carawan, "Singing and Shouting in Moving Star Hall," *Black Music Research Journal* 15, no. 1 (Spring 1995), 27–28.

96. Paper by Marion V. Kumar, "Negro Folklore" in Charles Perdue, *Don't Let the Devil Out-Talk You: Folk Songs, Rhymes, Chants, and Other Musical Material from the W.P.A. Collection of Ex-Slave Narratives,* unpublished paper from the University of Pennsylvania, 1970; in Georgia Collection, University of Georgia Library.

97. Parrish, *Slave Songs,* 54.

98. Parrish, *Slave Songs,* 55.

99. Alan Lomax in notes to *Georgia Sea Islands, Vol. 1,* Prestige/International LP 25001.

100. Conversation, July 1994.

101. Bruce Jackson, foreword to Folklore Associates edition of Parrish, *Slave Songs of the Georgia Sea Islands* (1965), xi.

102. Mary Arnold Twining, *An Examination of African Retentions in the Folk Culture of the South Carolina and Georgia Sea Islands* (Indiana University, Ph.D. diss., 1977), 144.

103. Interview, July 1981.

2. "One Family of People": The Shouters of Bolden

Buddy Sullivan, *Early Days on the Georgia Tidewater: The Story of McIntosh County and Sapelo* (McIntosh County, Ga.: Board of Commissioners, 1990). Reprinted from the *Savannah Morning News,* February 2, 1994.

1. Lawrence McKiver, interview, August 18, 1987.
2. Lawrence McKiver, interview, December 31, 1993.
3. Sullivan, *Early Days,* 215.
4. Ibid., 216–17.
5. Interview, August 18, 1987.
6. Interview, February 12, 1994.
7. Ibid.
8. Ibid.
9. Interview, August 18, 1987.
10. See Lorenzo Dow Turner, *Africanisms,* and *Drums and Shadows* for African language survivals in coastal Georgia.
11. McKiver's comments from interview in introduction to song, December 31, 1991.
12. Interview, August 8, 1983.
13. Ibid. For another recently collected Georgia version of this famous tale, see John Burrison, *Storytellers: Folktales and Legends from the South* (Athens: University of Georgia Press, 1989), 153–54; also, see Joel Chandler Harris, *Uncle Remus, His Songs and Sayings* (1895; reprint, New York: D. Appleton-Century, 1989), 7–11, 16–19.
14. Interview, August 18, 1987. See Richard Dorson, *Negro Folktales in Michigan* (Cambridge: Harvard University Press, 1956), for comments on this tale type.
15. Ibid.
16. Ibid.
17. Interview, February 12, 1994.
18. Interview, December 31, 1991.
19. Interview, July 15, 1995.
20. Interview, February 12, 1994.
21. Ibid.
22. James Holmes, *"Doctor Bullie's" Notes: Reminiscences of Early Georgia and of Philadelphia and New Haven in the 1800s,* ed. Delma Presley (Atlanta: Cherokee Publishing Company, 1976), 11.
23. Cook sang both the leader's calls and the gang's response punctuated by a plosive breath as the timbers had been shoved into place. He said that "the chantey would give you some energy to help you move the lumber and notify the other fel-

low how to pull down with you." Cook, born May 5, 1886, recalled that there were frequently as many as twenty-seven or twenty-eight four-masted schooners on the Darien riverfront at one time. His performance of this chantey, which we recorded September 5, 1981, can be heard on Folkways Records, FE 4344. Mary Arnold Twining collected a longer version of this chantey from John Davis of St. Simons Island, who also learned it when he worked as a stevedore in Darien (Twining, Ph.D. diss., 79–80).

24. Interview, February 12, 1994.

25. Ibid.

26. Interview, December 31, 1991.

27. Ibid.

28. Comments from Freddie Palmer and Carletha Sullivan from interview, February 12, 1994.

29. For a study of the past history and present situation of Sapelo Island's African American community, see William S. McFeely, *Sapelo's People: A Long Walk into Freedom* (New York: W. W. Norton, 1994).

30. Interview, July 15, 1995.

31. "A peculiarity of the African call-and-response pattern, found but infrequently elsewhere, is that the chorus' phrases regularly commence while the soloist is still singing; the leader, on his part, begins his phrase before the chorus has finished," Richard Waterman, "African Influence on the Music of the Americas," *Mother Wit from the Laughing Barrel,* ed. Alan Dundes (New York: Prentice-Hall, 1973), 88. Quoted in Thompson, *African Art,* 27.

32. Thompson, *African Art,* 27, 28.

33. Barre Toelken, "Ethnic Selection and Intensification in the Native American Powwow," in *Creative Ethnicity: Symbols and Strategies of Contemporary Ethnic Life,* Stephen Stern and John Allan Cicala, eds. (Logan: Utah State University Press, 1991).

34. Interview, February 12, 1994.

35. This conversation from interview, February 12, 1994.

36. Interview, December 1986.

37. Interview, February 12, 1994.

38. Interview, December 31, 1991.

39. Interview, February 12, 1994.

40. Henry Glassie, *Passing the Time in Ballymenone* (Pittsburgh: University of Pennsylvania Press, 1982), 33.

41. Interview, July 15, 1995.

42. Ibid.

43. Jones and Hawes, *Step It Down,* 144.

44. Folkways FE 4344, recorded and annotated by Art Rosenbaum, is currently available in cassette form and is sold by the shouters at public performances and even to visitors at the Watch Night Shout; "Down Yonder: The McIntosh County Shouters" was produced in 1986 by Clate Sanders of Georgia Public Television and is periodically rebroadcast in Georgia and beyond.

45. Interview, February 12, 1994.

46. Lee May, "The Art of Shouting," in the *Atlanta Journal-Constitution,* March 6, 1994.

47. Interview, July 29, 1994.

48. Ibid.

49. Interview, July 15, 1995.

3. Lawrence McKiver, Boss Songster

1. Interview, August 18, 1987.

2. Interview, February 12, 1994.

3. Interview, December 31, 1991.

4. See Jones and Hawes, *Step It Down,* for a full presentation of the ring play tradition. Bessie Jones used the same adjective as McKiver to characterize a well-performed play: "[The plays] are ceremonials, small testimonies to the ongoingness of life. . . . In order to be enjoyed properly . . . they must be done properly—that is, joyfully and humorously but with an underlying seriousness of intent to make it all come out right, to make, as Mrs. Jones says often and so touchingly, 'a beautiful play,'" xv.

5. This seems to be a variant of the better known game "Little Sally Walker." See Jones and Hawes, *Step It Down,* 107, and Art Rosenbaum, *Folk Visions and Voices: Traditional Music and Song in North Georgia* (Athens: University of Georgia Press, 1983), for a version collected from Doc and Lucy Barnes, 50–51.

6. Interview, December 31, 1991.

7. Interview, August 18, 1987.

8. Ibid.

9. Above from interview, February 12, 1994.

10. Interview, September 18, 1983.

11. Interview, August 18, 1987.

12. This is from another account of McKiver's fishing work, February 12, 1994.

13. Interview, August 18, 1987.

14. Ibid.

15. Ibid.

16. Ibid.

17. Interview, July 29, 1994.

18. Ibid.

19. Sung May 18, 1992.

20. Song and commentary, May 18, 1992.

21. McKiver is here alluding to diphthongs, not heard as commonly in the Gullah dialect as in other forms of spoken English. "Flat speech" may also refer to "level tones"; Alonso Dow Turner notes that, while Gullah has both rising and falling tones, "In Gullah . . . a level tone is quite common at the end of a question," where it would rise in standard English (Turner, *Africanisms,* 253). For more on the Gullah dialect, see Patricia Jones-Jackson, *When Roots Die: Endangered Traditions on the Sea Islands* (Athens: University of Georgia Press, 1987).

22. Interview, February 12, 1994.

23. Ibid.

Historical Essay. The Ring Shout: Revisiting the Islamic and African Issues of a Christian "Holy Dance"

1. Association of the term "shout" with African American musical genres, such as the "holler" or "field holler," should never arise. The ring shout emerged within the sacred context, while hollers emerged in the work song context.

2. I am indebted to Samuel A. Floyd, Jr., for this information regarding unpublished research that he had conducted on the ring shout.

3. Robert Winslow Gordon, "Negro 'Shouts' from Georgia," in *Mother Wit from the Laughing Barrel* (New York: Garland, 1981); Henry Edward Krehbiel, *Afro-American Folksongs* (New York: Frederick Unger, 1967); Courlander, *Negro Folk Music.*

4. Susan McClary and Robert Walser, "Theorizing the Body in African-American Music," *Black Music Research Journal* 14, no. 1:77.

5. Jay Rahn, "Turning the Analysis Around," *Black Music Research Journal* 16, no. 1:72–73.

6. Ibid., 74.

7. Allan D. Austin, *African Muslims in Antebellum America: A Sourcebook* (New York: Garland, 1984).

8. Abdulhafeez Q. Turkistani, "Muslim Slaves and their Narratives: Religious Faith and Cultural Accommodation" (Ph.D. diss., Kent State University).

9. Mary Twining, "Music, Movement, and Dance on the Sea Islands," *Black Music Research Journal* 15, no. 1:4.

10. Ibid.

Bibliography

This bibliography consolidates works used by the author and those used by Johann Buis in his essay on Islamic and African issues related to the ring shout. Works used and/or cited by Johann S. Buis are designated (J. S. B.). Those used by both writers are designated (A. R., J. S. B.). All others, without designations, are those works used only by Rosenbaum.

Abrahams, Roger D. *Singing the Master: The Emergence of African American Culture in the Plantation South*. New York: Pantheon Books, 1992.

Allen, Roy. "Shouting the Church: Narrative and Vocal Improvisation in African-American Gospel Quartet Performance." *Journal of American Folklore*, vol. 104, no. 413 (Summer 1991).

Allen, William Francis, Charles Pickard Ware, Lucy McKim Garrison. *Slave Songs of the United States* (1867). New edition, with new introduction by W. K. McNeil. Baltimore: Clearfield Co., 1992.

Austin, Allan D. *African Muslims in Antebellum America: A Sourcebook*. New York: Garland, 1984. (J. S. B.)

Ball, Charles. *Slavery in the United States: A Narrative of the Life and Adventures of Charles Ball, a Black Man, Who Lived Forty Years in Maryland, South Carolina and Georgia as a Slave*. New York: J. S. Taylor, 1837.

Barry, Phillips. "Negro Folk-Songs from Maine: The Shout." *Bulletin of the Folk Song Society of the Northeast* 9 (1935). Reprint, Philadelphia: American Folklore Society, 1960.

Blesh, Rudi, and Harriet Janis. *They All Played Ragtime*. New York: Alfred A. Knopf, 1950. Rev. ed., New York: Oak Publications, 1966.

Bolton, Dorothy G. *Old Songs Hymnal: Words and Melodies from the State of Georgia*. New York: Century Co., 1929.

Bravermann, René A. *Islam and Tribal Art in West Africa*. London: Cambridge University Press, 1974. (J. S. B.)

Brewer, J. Mason. *American Negro Folklore.* Chicago: Quadrangle Books, 1968.

Brown, Scott E. *James P. Johnson: A Case of Mistaken Identity.* Metuchen, N.J.: Scarecrow Press and the Institute of Jazz Studies, Rutgers University, 1982.

Buis, Johann S. "African Slave Descendants in an American Community: The Ringshout Tradition of the Georgia Sea Islands. An African Outsider Looks In." *Proceedings of the 1994 Seminar of the Commission on Community Music, International Society for Music Education,* Mary Legar, ed. Athens, Ga.: p.u., 1994. (J. S. B.)

Burrison, John. *Storytellers: Folktales and Legends from the South.* Athens: University of Georgia Press, 1989.

Carawan, Guy, and Candie Carawan. *Ain't You Got a Right to the Tree of Life.* New York: Simon and Schuster, 1966; rev. and expanded ed. Athens: University of Georgia Press, 1989.

Carawan, Guy, with Candie Carawan. "Singing and Shouting in Moving Star Hall." *Black Music Research Journal* 15, no. 1 (Spring 1995).

Chernoff, John Miller. *African Rhythm and African Sensibility: Aesthetics and Social Action in African Musical Idioms.* Chicago: University of Chicago Press, 1979. (A. R., J. S. B.)

Clarke, Erskine. *Wrestlin' Jacob.* Atlanta: John Knox Press, 1979.

Conrad, Georgia Bryan. *Reminiscences of a Southern Woman.* Hampton Institute Press, [n.d.].

Courlander, Harold. *Negro Folk Music, U.S.A.* New York: Columbia University Press, 1963. (A. R., J. S. B.)

Crouther, Betty J. "Iconography of Henry Gudgell Walking Stick." *Southeastern College Art Conference Review* 12, no. 3 (1993).

David, Jonathan. *On One Accord: Singing and Praying Bands of Tidewater Maryland and Delaware.* Notes to Global Village CD 225. New York: Global Village Music, 1992.

Dorson, Richard. *Negro Folktales in Michigan.* Cambridge: Harvard University Press, 1956.

Emery, Lynne Fauley. *Black Dance from 1919 to Today.* Rev. ed., Pennington, N.J.: Princeton Book Co., 1988.

Epstein, Dena J. *Sinful Tunes and Spirituals: Black Folk Music to the Civil War.* Urbana: University of Illinois Press, 1977.

Farmer, Henry G. *A History of Arabian Music to the Thirteenth Century.* London, Eng.: Luzac, 1967. (J. S. B.)

Fisher, Miles Mark. *Negro Slave Songs in the United States.* New York: Citadel Press, 1953.

Forten, Charlotte. *Life on Sea Islands*. 1864.

Genovese, Eugene D. *Roll, Jordan, Roll: The World the Slaves Made*. New York: Pantheon Books, 1972.

Georgia Writers' Project (Savannah Unit), Works Project Administration. *Drums and Shadows: Survival Studies Among the Georgia Coastal Negroes*. Reprint, Athens: University of Georgia Press, 1940. (A. R., J. S. B.)

Glassie, Henry. *Passing the Time in Ballymenone*. Pittsburgh: University of Pennsylvania Press, 1982.

Gordon, Robert W. "Negro 'Shouts' from Georgia." *Mother Wit from the Laughing Barrel*. New York: Garland, 1981. (A. R., J. S. B.)

Gordon, Robert W. "The Negro Spiritual." *Carolina Low Country,* Augustine T. Smythe, Herbert Ravenel Sass, et al. New York: Macmillan, 1931.

Harris, Joel Chandler. *Uncle Remus, His Songs and Sayings* (1895). Reprint, New York: D. Appleton-Century, 1989.

Haskins, James. *Black Dance in America: A History Through Its People*. New York: Harper Collins, 1990. (J. S. B.)

Hawley, Thomas Earl, Jr. *The Slave Tradition of Singing Among the Gullah of Johns Island, South Carolina*. Ph.D. diss., University of Maryland, 1993.

Higginson, Thomas Wentworth. *Army Life in a Black Regiment*. Boston: Fields, Osgood, 1870.

Holmes, James. *"Doctor Bullie's" Notes: Reminiscences of Early Georgia and Philadelphia and New Haven in the 1800s,* Delma Presley, ed. Atlanta: Cherokee Publishing Company, 1976.

Jackson, Bruce. *The Negro and His Folklore in Nineteenth-Century Periodicals*. Austin: University of Texas Press, 1967.

Jackson, George Pullen. *White Spirituals in the Southern Uplands*. Chapel Hill: University of North Carolina Press, 1933.

Jenkins, Jean, and Poul Olsen. *Music and Musical Instruments in the World of Islam*. London: World of Islam Festival Publishers, 1976. (J. S. B.)

Johnson, Guion Griffis. *A Social History of the Sea Islands*. Chapel Hill: University of North Carolina Press, 1930.

Johnson, James Weldon. *The Book of American Negro Spirituals*. New York: Viking Press, 1925.

Johnson, James Weldon. *The Second Book of Negro Spirituals*. New York: Viking Press, 1926.

Jones, Bessie, and Bess Lomax Hawes. *Step it Down: Games, Plays, Songs, and Stories from the Afro-American Heritage*. New York: Harper and Row, 1972.

Joyner, Charles W. *Folk Song in South Carolina*. Columbia: University of South Carolina Press, 1971.

Katz, Bernard, ed. *The Social Implications of Early Negro Music in the United States*. New York: Arno Press, 1969.

Krehbiel, Henry Edward. *Afro-American Folksongs: A Study in Racial and National Music*. New York: G. Schirmer, 1914. (A. R., J. S. B.)

Lincoln, C. Eric, and Lawrence H. Mamiya. *The Black Church in the African American Experience*. Durham: Duke University Press, 1990.

Lomax, Alan. *The Folk Songs of North America*. Garden City, N.Y.: Doubleday, 1960.

Lomax, Alan. *Georgia Sea Islands, Vol. 2*. Notes to Prestige/International LP 25001.

Lyell, Sir Charles. *A Second Visit to the United States of North America*. New York: Harper & Brothers, 1849.

Marks, Morton. "Uncovering Ritual Structures in Afro-American Music." *Religious Movements in Contemporary America,* Irving I. Zaretsky and Mark P. Leone, eds. Princeton: Princeton University Press, 1974.

Marshall, Lorna. "Kung Bushmen Religious Beliefs." *Africa* 2 (1962).

McClary, Susan, and Robert Walser. "Theorizing the Body in African-American Music." *Black Music Research Journal* 14, no. 1:77. (J. S. B.)

McFeely, William S. *Sapelo's People: A Long Walk into Freedom*. New York: W. W. Norton, 1994.

McIlhenny, E. A. *Befo' the War Spirituals*. Boston: Christopher, 1933.

Montgomery, Michael, ed. *The Crucible of Carolina: Essays in the Development of Gullah Language and Culture*. Athens: The University of Georgia Press, 1994.

Nichols, Elaine, ed. *The Last Miles of the Way: African-American Homegoing Traditions, 1890–Present*. Columbia: South Carolina State Museum, 1989.

Odum, Howard W., and Guy B. Johnson. *The Negro and His Songs,* Chapel Hill: University of North Carolina Press, 1925.

Parrish, Lydia. *Slave Songs of the Georgia Sea Islands* (1942). 1965 Reprint with foreword by Bruce Jackson, Folklore Associates; 1992 reprint with foreword by Art Rosenbaum, Athens: University of Georgia Press. (A. R., J. S. B.)

Payne, Bishop Daniel Alexander. *Recollections of Seventy Years* (1883). Reprint, New York: Arno Press and the *New York Times,* 1968.

Perdue, Charles. *Don't Let the Devil Out-Talk You: Folk Songs, Rhymes, Chants, and Other Musical Material from the W.P.A. Collection of Folklore and Ex-Slave Narratives*. Unpublished paper, University of Pennsylvania, 1970. In Georgia Collection, University of Georgia Library.

Plair, Sally. *Something to Shout About: Reflections on the Gullah Spiritual*. Mount Pleasant, S.C.: Molasses Lane Publishers, 1972.

Puckett, Newbell Niles. *Folk Beliefs of the Southern Negro.* Chapel Hill: University of North Carolina Press, 1926.

Raboteau, Albert J. *Slave Religion: The "Invisible Institution" in the Antebellum South.* Oxford: Oxford University Press, 1978.

Rahn, Jay. "Turning the Analysis Around." *Black Music Research Journal* 16, no. 1: 72–73. (J. S. B.)

Rosenbaum, Art. *The McIntosh County Shouters: Slave Shout Songs from the Coast of Georgia.* Notes to Folkways Records LP 4344. New York: Folkways Records and Service Corp., 1984. (A. R., J. S. B.)

Smiley, P. "Folk-Lore from Va., S.C., Ga., Ala., and Fla." *Journal of American Folklore* 32 (1919), 378.

Sobel, Mechal. *Trabelin' On: The Slave Journey to an Afro-Baptist Faith.* Westport, Conn.: Greenwood Press, 1979.

Speck, Frank G. "Ethnology of the Yuchi Indians." Philadelphia: University Museum, *Anthropological Publications, University of Pennsylvania, Vol. 1,* 1909.

Spencer, Jon Michael. *Protest and Praise: Sacred Music of Black Religion.* Minneapolis, Minn.: Augsburg Fortress, 1990. (J. S. B.)

Stuckey, Sterling. *Slave Culture: Nationalist Theory and the Foundations of Black America.* New York: Oxford University Press, 1987. (A. R., J. S. B.)

Sullivan, Buddy. *Early Days on the Georgia Tidewater: The Story of McIntosh County & Sapelo.* McIntosh County: Board of Commissioners, 1990.

Thompson, Robert Farris. *African Art in Motion.* Los Angeles: University of California Press, 1974.

Thompson, Robert Farris. *Flash of the Spirit: African and Afro-American Art and Philosophy.* New York: Random House, 1983.

Tirro, Frank. *Jazz: A History.* New York: W. W. Norton, 1977.

Toelken, Barre. "Ethnic Selection and Intensification in the Native American Powwow." *Creative Ethnicity: Symbols and Strategies of Contemporary Ethnic Life,* Stephen Stern and Johan Allan Cicala, eds. Logan: Utah State University Press, 1991.

Tschakert, Irmgard. *Wandlungen persischer Tanzmusikgattungen unter westlichem Einfluss. Beitraege zur Ethnomusikologie,* vol. 2. Hamburg: Verlag der Musikhandlungen Karl Dieter Wagner, 1972. (J. S. B.)

Turkistani, Abdulhafeez Q. "Muslim Slaves and Their Narratives: Religious Faith and Cultural Accommodation." Ph.D. diss., Kent State University, 1996. (J. S. B.)

Turner, Lorenzo Dow. *Africanisms in the Gullah Dialect.* Ann Arbor: University of Michigan Press, 1949.

Twining, Mary Arnold. *An Examination of African Retentions in the Folk Culture of the South Carolina and Georgia Sea Islands.* Ph.D. diss., Indiana University, 1977.

Twining, Mary Arnold. "Music, Movement, and Dance on the Sea Islands." *Black Music Research Journal* 15, no. 1:4. (J. S. B.)

Twining, Mary Arnold, and Keith Baird, eds. *Sea Island Roots: African Presence in the Carolinas and Georgia.* Trenton, N.J.: African World Press, 1991. (J. S. B.)

Waterman, Richard. "African Influence on the Music of the Americas." *Mother Wit from the Laughing Barrel,* ed. Alan Dundes. New York: Prentice-Hall, 1973.

Wilson, Olly. "The Significance of the Relationship Between Afro-American Music and West-African Music." *Black Perspective in Music* 2, no. 1 (Spring 1974): 3–22. (J. S. B.)

Woofter, T. J., Jr. *Black Yeomanry: Life on St. Helena Island.* New York: Octagon Books, 1978.

Work, John W. *American Negro Songs and Spirituals.* New York: Bonanza Books, 1940.

Index

Abrahams, Roger, 26
Allen, William Francis, xiii, xiv, 22, 27, 29, 31–33, 34
Asch, Moe, xii

Baldwin, James, 45
Barry, Phillips, 46–48
Bremer, Fredrika, 26
Brown, Katie, 36
Brown, William Wells, 37
Bryant, Reverend, 9
Buis, Johann, xiii, 3

Campbell, Catherine, 1, 34, 75
Carawan, Candie, xiii
Carawan, Guy, xiii, 48, 49
Conrad, Georgia Bryan, 25
Cook, Deacon James: on the shout, 2, 4, 5, 6, 52, 68, 75; on oldest slave song, 18; sings chantey, 67
Cook, Nathan, 52
Courlander, Harold, 20, 23

David, Jonathan, 38, 39

Ector, Bettye, ix, x, 71, 75, 80; on reasons for continuing shout, 70; on "showmanship," 79
Ellison, Oneitha, 55, 75, 81
Ellison, Thelma, 66, 75
Emmett, Dan, 37

Epstein, Dena, xiii
Evans, Charlotte, 86, 98
Evans, Fannie Ann, 33, 91–92
Evans, Harold, 8

Forten, Charlotte, 35
Fussell, Fred, 2

Gannett, Edward Channing, 37
Garrison, Lucy McKim, 27
Glassie, Henry, 78
Gordon, Robert W., xiii, 42–44, 47

Hawes, Bess Lomax, 11, 80
Higginson, Thomas Wentworth, 27, 28, 35
Holloway, Lucille, 106
Hopkins, Charles, 54
Hurston, Zora Neale, 45, 50

Jackson, Bruce, 51
Jackson, George Pullen, 47
Jackson, Reverend Leonard, 7
Jenkins, Amy, 55, 56, 68, 75, 106
Jenkins, London, 55, 56, 68, 75, 106
Johnson, James P., 44–45
Johnson, James Weldon, 40–41
Jones, Bessie, 80
Jones, Charles Colcock, 22

Kingston, Jack, 81
Krehbiel, Henry Edward, 37, 47

Lomax, Alan, xiii, 26, 50, 105
Lomax, John, 26, 105
Lyell, Sir Charles, 24

McCullough, Bo, 91
McIver, Venus, x, 78, 84
McIver, Vertie, x, xv, 4, 69, 75, 79
McKiver, Lawrence, ix, 2, 5, 6, 7–8, 9,
    10–12, 17, 18, 33, 36, 52, 54, 71, 75,
    80, 81, 85, 86, 103–4, 106, 107; on
    slavery times, 56–57; tells slave folk
    tales, 58–60; on community folklife,
    60–61; on the ring shout, 61–62,
    64–65, 68–69, 78, 85, 90–92, 101–3;
    praises houses and churches, 62–64;
    on call-and-response in the shout,
    72–73; organizes McIntosh County
    Shouters, 74; on public performance
    of shout, 75–77; early memories
    of, 86–89; on childhood ring plays,
    89–90; on dances and frolics, 92–94;
    work as fisherman, 94–96; on herbal
    cures, 96; wife and children of, 96;
    on "haints" (ghosts), 97; on army
    service and racial incident, 98;
    church membership, choir, and
    original songs of, 99–101; on
    "Geechee" dialect, 101
Mitchell, George, 2

Nephew, Ishmael, 67
Nichols, Elaine, 19–20

Palmer, Anna Mae, 96
Palmer, Deacon Andrew, 75, 81
Palmer, Deacon Freddie, 8, 12, 55, 56,
    67, 70, 76; on the ring shout, 65–66,
    82–84
Palmer, Deacon Joseph, 62–63
Palmer, Martha, 55

Palmer, Reverend Nathan, x, 6, 7–8,
    10, 54, 66, 70, 86
Parrish, Lydia, xiii, xiv, 2, 37, 50
Payne, Bishop Daniel Alexander,
    38–39
Perdue, Charles, 49

Quarterman, Wallace, 36
Quimby, Doug, xii, 2, 74
Quimby, Frankie, xii, 2, 51, 74

Raboteau, Albert J., 21–22
Reed, Benjamin, x, xiv, 8, 11, 78, 81
Rivers, Prince, 35

Sanders, Clate, xii, xiv, 5
Schlesinger, Michael, 40
Skipper, Doretha, 6, 7, 12, 75
Smith, Willie "the Lion," 44
Spaulding, Henry George, 31
Sullivan, Carletha, ix, x, 13, 54, 55, 56,
    66, 68, 77–78, 81; on the shout, 66,
    82–84; hollering, 66; on local
    economy, 70

Temple, Elizabeth, 75
Thompson, Robert Farris, 18–19, 34,
    72
Toelken, Barre, 73
Tomlinson, Reuben, 35
Towne, Laura, 34
Turner, Lorenzo Dow, 3
Twining, Mary Arnold, 51

Ware, Charles Pickard, 27
Woofter, T. J., 48
Wylly, Alexander William, 54

Young, Odessa, ix, 71, 75 ; on the shout,
    64, 76, 78–79